Contents

Preface

This new book explores in a very lucid and informative way a range of issues concerned with the influences on business organisation strategies and how business organisations draw up, implement and evaluate their strategies.

Corporate strategy is crucial in determining whether a business organisation achieves its objectives. The importance of corporate strategy is recognised in the new A level and VCE specifications, HND and degree courses. The book should prove to be a valuable resource for students studying for AQA's AS level Module 3 and A level Module 6, Edexcel's AS Unit 1 and A level Unit 6 and OCR's AS Module 2871 and A level Module 2880.

The author, Rob Dransfield, is a senior lecturer in Economics and Business Studies at the Nottingham Trent University, and has wide experience in the areas of teaching, examining and industry. He is also a well-known and respected writer in the fields of business studies and economics. Among the books he has written is *Human Resource Management*, a popular title in this series.

Sue Grant
Series Editor

Corporate Strategy

Rob Dransfield

Series Editor
Susan Grant
West Oxfordshire College

Heinemann

Heinemann Educational Publishers
Halley Court, Jordan Hill, Oxford OX2 8EJ
a division of Reed Educational and Professional Publishing Ltd

OXFORD MELBOURNE   AUCKLAND
JOHANNESBURG   BLANTYRE   GABARONE   IBADAN
PORTSMOUTH (NH) USA   CHICAGO

Heinemann is a registered trademark of Reed Educational and
Professional Publishing Ltd

First published in 2001

05 04 03 02 01
10 9 8 7 6 5 4 3 2 1

Tw

658.401 DRA

EG 15808

British Library Cataloguing in Publication Data

ISBN 0435 33220 1

Typeset and illustrated by Techtype Ltd
Printed and bound in Great Britain by Biddles Ltd, Guildford

Acknowledgements
The publishers would like to thank the following for permission to
reproduce copyright material:

The Independent for the articles on pp. 4, 52, 78 and 97; The *Financial
Times* for the article on p. 25; Anna Crow, Caroline Slaney and Debra
Morton for providing the case study on Marks and Spencer; Ross
Mason for providing the case study on the Co-operative Bank.

Introduction

The most successful organisations – Oxfam, Manchester United, Coca-Cola, Microsoft, Nestlé, Cadbury-Schweppes, Heinz, and many others – all place a high priority on having clear and well thought out organisational plans. We call the major plans of these organisations corporate strategies because they are designed to enable the management of the whole organisation. These strategies are the means which enable organisations to achieve their objectives. For the business organisations listed above a key part of their strategy is to dominate the global market in the goods and services which they are renowned for – whether they be football related entertainment, soft drinks or computers. Not-for-profit organisations like Oxfam have different aims and purposes related to providing for the needy wherever they may be. However, whatever type of organisation we are looking at there is a need for a clear sense of direction and a plan to achieve goals and objectives.

Corporate strategies are shaped by managers' understanding of the relationship between the organisation and its environment. A key part of strategic management is seeking to create the best possible fit between the resources and competences of an organisation, the structure of the organisation, and the external environment. Today, organisational environments are more turbulent than ever before, being characterised by intense competition (often on a global scale), rapid changes in technology, and many other dynamic factors. Indeed business writers frequently feel that we are living on the edge of chaos. Strategy therefore needs to be highly flexible if it is to be able to cope with decision making in the modern world. The organisation that fails to adapt to its environment will go the way of the dinosaurs.

Of course, strategy is not just the concern of large multinational businesses, rather it is the concern of all organisations. The purpose of strategy is to enable the organisation to make its own future rather than simply to react to changes that take place around it.

All students need to have a good understanding of corporate strategy because not only does it enable them to understand how the plans of organisations are shaped, it also provides them with a framework for helping to shape the future plans of organisations when they take on managerial roles.

Students will need to read further, using the references recommended at the end of each chapter as well as the various websites. In addition, students can keep up to date by seeking articles about corporate strategy in newspapers such as *The Independent* and the *Financial Times*, as well as reading articles in specialist journals such as the *McKinsey Quarterly* and *Organisational Dynamics*.

Chapter 1 gives a brief outline of the nature of corporate strategy and sets out a map of Chapters 2-7 showing the key parts of an ordered planning framework.

Chapter 2 shows how strategies need to be shaped by the past successes of an organisation.

Chapter 3 outlines procedures involved in scanning the external environment of the organisation to outline key changes in the wider political, economic, social, technological, legal and environmental influences as well as in the competitive environment.

Chapter 4 explains the importance of identifying the internal strengths and weaknesses of an organisation and the external threats and opportunities facing the organisation in helping to formulate strategies.

Chapter 5 outlines the importance of defining the purpose and objectives of the organisation. It shows the importance of knowing what you stand for and what you want to achieve.

Chapter 6 is concerned with identifying a range of generic and competitive strategies for the organisation. It examines a range of major types of strategy which are typical of those being pursued by modern organisations.

Chapter 7 highlights ways in which the organisation can implement its strategy and ways in which it can then monitor and evaluate ongoing strategies. It shows that, in a dynamic business environment, the strategy that emerges may be different from what was originally planned.

Chapter 8 examines ways in which managers can plan strategic change in an organisation and overcome the barriers which exist.

Chapter 9 identifies globalisation as a key strategy that is being pursued by many large organisations today – both as a means of expanding their sphere of interests and profits, and as a means of defending against the actions of competitors.

A set of case studies with discussion points is provided at the end of the text, focusing on key learning points.

Chapter One

What is corporate strategy?

'Strategy has traditionally been a high-stakes game that starts when a management team develops a vision of the company's future environment. The team then makes big, hard-to-reverse decisions about where the company will focus its energies, its capital, and its people. Finally, the team hopes and prays that its vision is correct.'
Eric D. Beinhocker

An organisation's strategies are its long-term plans which will help it to achieve its objectives in a changing environment.

It is important to understand how businesses create and make use of **corporate strategies**.

Definitions	
Corporate	Involving the whole of the organisation/business
Strategy	Major long-term plans

Strategies are the means through which organisations are able to achieve the **objectives** that they set for themselves. Objectives are the desired results that the organisation seeks to achieve. Some strategies will be successful while others will fail to deliver the desired results.

An example of a recent strategy which was highlighted in the press was that of Ryanair which has set itself the objective of expanding its capacity to 14 million passengers by 2004 and to become the number five airline in Europe. The airline has a low-cost, low-fare strategy. In February 2001, the company placed 10 million new shares enabling it to buy new planes so that it could operate on more routes.

Strategic management

Developing corporate strategies is a management responsibility (largely involving senior managers). **Strategic management** decisions made by managers at the top of the organisation trigger dozens or even hundreds of other decisions of lesser magnitude made by lower level managers in the organisation. If the strategies created by senior managers are inappropriate then this will lead to ineffective choices being made at all levels within the organisation.

Ryanair chief O'Leary to cash in £30m shares as airline raises funds to expand

Michael O'Leary, chief executive of Ryanair, the no-frills airline, said yesterday that the carrier would be carrying more passengers than British Airways within a decade.

Mr O'Leary also announced that he will collect up to £30m through the sale of 3 million Ryanair shares from his personal holding. At the same time the company is placing 10 million new shares to raise about £79m. Each of the sales could be boosted by 1 million additional shares, if there is sufficient demand. The company will use the funds to buy new planes, principally 13 Boeing 737–800 aircraft, to be delivered between December this year and January 2003.

Mr O'Leary would not specify how he planned to spend the money he will personally raise. He said only that it was not sensible to have almost the whole of his wealth tied up in the airline. Outside Ryanair, his main interest is a farm outside Dublin where he raises cattle.

The company's 1997 floatation left him with a 12 per cent stake, which he has been progressively selling down. After the divestment announced yesterday, he will be left with 7.5 per cent stake, worth about £250m.

Ryanair yesterday reported a 23 per cent jump in pre-tax profit to 24.3m euros (£15.6m) for the third quarter to 30 December. Passenger numbers grew, compared with the third quarter of the previous year, from 1.39 million to 1.89 million.

The airline said that before the end of the month, it will announce six new destinations, one additional European base and increased frequency on some of its existing routes. The expansion is designed to enable Ryanair's capacity to grow to 9 million passengers over the coming year. Mr O'Leary said that the airline would double in size to 14 million passenger by 2004. This would make it the number five player in Europe – behind BA, Air France, Luftansa and KLM. Ryanair's first scheduled flight was in 1986. He added: 'At this rate we will be bigger than BA in eight years, making us Europe's biggest international airline.' On Monday BA reported third-quarter opening margins of 3.5 per cent, compared with Ryanair's latest margins of 19 per cent.

Chris Tarry, an analyst at Commerzbank, said that yesterday's results showed that Ryanair's business model was 'genuinely low-cost, rather than just low fare'. Operating costs rose in the quarter by 29 per cent but passengers carried grew by 39 per cent. Marketing and distribution expenses dropped by 66 per cent, as direct bookings accounted for 90 per cent of business. Mr O'Leary said that the airline's growth rate, running at 25 per cent a year, could be sustained for the next 15 or 20 years, without needing to go beyond Europe. The company's shares closed down 15p to 754p.

The Independent, 7 February 2001, by Saeed Shah

> **Definition**
> A **decision** is made when a decision maker selects a particular course of action (rather than alternatives). The decision is made because this is seen as the best way of achieving objectives (ideally after an ongoing process of carefully evaluating the alternatives)

Decision making is the most important activity carried out by managers in all types of organisations and at any level of management. Indeed it is decision making that distinguishes managers from other occupations in society.

Strategic decisions are highly complex and involve a host of dynamic variables. These decisions are highly significant because they deal with the long-term health of the organisation.

Strategic management involves four processes.

- **Understanding** – the strategic situation in which the organisation is placed. This involves carrying out a **strategic audit** – i.e. a process of researching and understanding the total business environment. Understanding also involves finding out about the market place, and about competitors.
- **Formulation** – choosing suitable strategies for the organisation. The first stage here is to decide on the future direction of the organisation. This involves defining the aim of the organisation which is termed the **mission**. It is also important to agree on the **values** of the organization, i.e. what it stands for and the way in which the organisation and its people should behave. With the mission and values in place it is possible to decide on the **strategies** to be pursued to achieve the chosen aims.

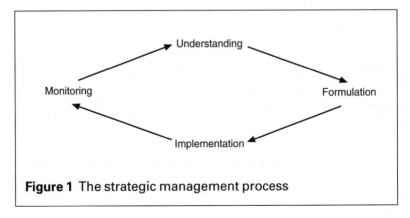

Figure 1 The strategic management process

Corporate _ _ _ _ _ _ _ _ _ _ _	The organisation-wide plan dealing with the long-term health of the whole organisation
Competitive _ _ _ _ _ _ _ _ _ _	Concerned with seeking and gaining a competitive advantage over rivals
Functional _ _ _ _ _ _ _ _ _ _ _	Identifying and applying competitive strategies in functional areas

Figure 2 Interlinked levels of strategy

- **Implementation** – making the chosen strategies happen. This involves putting into practice the chosen strategies at all the various levels within the organisation.
- **Monitoring** – checking and evaluating the success of the chosen strategies, in order to make adjustments where necessary.

Developing corporate strategy is an ongoing rather than a one-off process. Managers would rarely develop a strategy from scratch (except in the case of a start-up business). At any one time an organisation will be working with a set of strategies – some of which are more successful than others. Devising strategy usually involves deciding whether to continue with existing strategies, or to devise a series of new strategies to take the organisation into the future.

There are thus three linked levels of strategic management – corporate strategy, competitive strategy and functional strategy.

Crafting strategy

Henry Mintzberg (1987) argues that it is helpful to think of strategy as being crafted (**crafting strategy**). He uses the metaphor of the potter at work. 'The potter sits before a lump of clay on the wheel. Her mind is on the clay, but she is also aware of sitting between her past experiences and her future prospects. She knows exactly what has and has not worked for her in the past. She has an intimate knowledge of her work, her capabilities, and her markets. As a craft worker, she senses rather than analyses these things; her knowledge is 'tacit.' All these things are working in her mind as her hands are working the clay. The product that emerges on the wheel is likely to be in the tradition of her past work, but she may break away and embark on a new direction. Even so, the past is no less present, projecting itself into the future.'

In Mintzberg's metaphor, managers are craft workers and strategy is their clay. They sit between the past of corporate capabilities (what the organisation has done and is able to do and achieve), and a future of market opportunities. The true craft worker will bring to their work an intimate knowledge of the materials at hand (the resources and key strengths of the organisation).

Competitive strategies

An effective strategy is one that enables an organisation to achieve its objectives and will need to be based on each of the following characteristics:

- It should be sustainable – once established it should be able to run and be able to be built on over time.
- Distinctive from competitors – the strategy should set out to help the organisation and its activities to be different from rivals.
- Enable an organisation to gain a competitive advantage.
- It should exploit links between the organisation and its environment. Organisations need to change and adapt to the environment, and make effective links with the environment – for example by developing close links with customers.
- It should be based on a vision that enables the organisation to develop better links with the environment – for example, helping the organisation to move into bigger and better markets.

Michael Porter (1998) argues that **competitive strategy** involves being different – 'It means deliberately choosing a different set of activities to deliver a unique mix of values'. He states that in recent years many companies have mistaken operational efficiency for strategy. They have set out to carry out their activities in a highly efficient way often by following the best practice of their rivals. However, this does not translate into high levels of profitability – because competitors are doing exactly the same thing.

Competitive strategy therefore involves being excellent at everything you do while at the same time concentrating on being different from rivals.

John Thompson (1995) defines competitive strategy as being 'concerned with creating and maintaining a **competitive advantage** (superiority over rivals) in each and every area of the business'. For each functional part of a business (e.g. marketing, finance and accounts, etc.) there will need to be a strategy – but these strategies will be part of a co-ordinated whole (**functional strategies**).

Key steps in strategic planning

Strategies enable an organisation to build on its past, plan for the future and to monitor ongoing progress. In order to carry out this process in

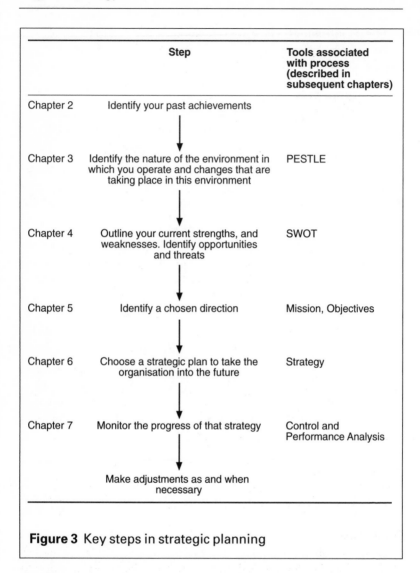

Figure 3 Key steps in strategic planning

an organised sequence it is helpful to carry out a number of steps which are summarised in Fig. 3 (and which follow the next few chapters). It is helpful to keep referring back to the diagram to see where each aspect of strategy that you are studying fits into the overall picture.

KEY WORDS	
Corporate strategies	Values
Objectives	Strategies
Strategic management	Implementation
Decisions	Monitoring
Understanding	Crafting strategy
Strategic audit	Competitive strategies
Formulation	Competitive advantage
Mission	Functional strategies

Further reading

Greenley, G., Chapter 1, *Strategic Management*, Prentice Hall, 1999.

Needham, D., Dransfield, R., *et al*, Chapter 28, *Business for Higher Awards*, second edition, Heinemann, 1999.

Thompson J.L., Chapter 1, *Strategic Management*, Thomson Business Press, 2000.

Thompson J.L., Chapter 1, *Strategy in Action*, Chapman & Hall, 1995.

Additional references

Mintzberg, H., Crafting strategy, in *The Strategy Process*, ed. Mintzberg, H., Prentice Hall, 1996.

Porter, M., What is strategy? Chapter 4, in ed. Segal-Horn, S., *The Strategy Reader*, Blackwell Business, 1998.

Useful websites

IBM website: www.ibm.com

Ryanair website: www.ryanair.com

Essay topics

1. What do you understand by the term corporate strategy?   [5 marks]
   How does the development of a strategy enable an organisation to achieve its objectives?   [5 marks]
   Explain how the development of corporate strategy is an ongoing process.   [10 marks]
2. How can corporate strategy be employed to help an organisation to gain a competitive advantage over rivals?   [20 marks]

Data response question – Changing the nature of IBM

IBM was the best known name in information and communications technology in the twentieth century, and IBM products and services came with the IBM name stamped on them – on servers, computers, software packages, etc.

However, in the post-millennium period, with the rise of the networked world, the PC era is coming to an end, and a smaller percentage of customers will buy an item with 'IBM' stamped on it. New technologies are being developed which will give customers access to the Internet through other media such as television sets and WAP phones.

At the same time more and more businesses are developing websites and engaging in a range of e-commerce activities. Mobile applications are becoming a major force for delivering e-business in Europe.

As an organisation with huge resources IBM has decided to change the way it carries out business in order to better place itself to be competitive in this new world. IBM customers (including many existing and new companies) are seeking help to develop new links with customers using the Internet. For example, they want to develop the best possible websites enabling them to carry out market research, to show their goods and services to customers, and to build good relationships with customers.

IBM therefore has radically altered its business to concentrate on helping other companies to create links with the Internet by creating the most appropriate systems.

IBM is able to do this because they already have more experience in this field than anybody. IBM has many gifted information technology specialists working for them with a wealth of experience in creating websites and creating systems for e-business.

In the future therefore IBM's presence will not only come through products and services stamped 'IBM' but also using the benefits of IBM's innovative technology, much of it will be inside other companies' branded products, or at work behind the scenes in the computing infrastructure of the net.

By 2005 half of IBM's revenues and workforce will come from services. IBM has therefore refocused a large part of its activity on creating e-business, i.e. in helping customers to use the latest technology to maximum advantage.

1. How can the move by IBM from 'IBM' stamped products to the provision of e-business services for other companies be described as corporate strategy? [3 marks]
2. Who would have been responsible for creating this change in strategy? [2 marks]
3. How is the change in emphasis at IBM also an example of competitive strategy? [3 marks]
4. To what extent is the change in strategy at IBM made possible because of the past achievements of the corporation? [7 marks]
5. What steps would IBM need to take to ensure the ongoing success of the new strategy? [5 marks]

Chapter Two

Identifying past achievements

'Defining a business in terms of what it is capable of doing may offer a more durable basis for strategy than a definition based upon the needs which the business seeks to satisfy.'   Robert M. Grant

All businesses except the very new have come from somewhere – they have a history. In devising a strategy it is important to take stock of those past achievements which are likely to be important in determining the organisation's ability to proceed into the future.

For example, the Coca-Cola Company is perhaps the best known global brand in the world. The company has come a long way since the product was invented in 1886 by Dr John Styth Pemberton in a back yard in Atlanta, Georgia. Coca-Cola has been successful largely because it has been able to differentiate its product from rivals, partly through taste but more importantly through image, e.g. the classic shape of its bottles, the way in which its logo has become an advertising icon, and the strength of its advertising to the young and fashion conscious. It was Coca-Cola that transformed Santa Claus' robes into their red and white colours to support one of their advertising campaigns. Today, the company is selling over 1 billion servings a day. There are very few countries where Coca-Cola is not sold, and most consumers are aware of the Coca-Cola drink. Over the years the company has spent billions of pounds on advertising and on brand promotion. As a result of the success of its global marketing strategy, Coca-Cola has been able to win substantial profits which it can then plough back into the business, for example in purchasing new resources such as new plant and top-quality employees (such as high-quality creative marketing executives). The Coca-Cola success story is based as much on its' past achievements as it is on its determination to continually seek new markets and opportunities in the 21st century.

Past achievements will affect the organisation's:

- **Reputation** (what people think of the organisation).
- **Profitability**.
- **Resources** (inputs into the production process) available to the organization.
- **Capabilities** of the organisation. A capability is the capacity for a team of resources to perform some task or activity. Productive

How Nokia built on its past achievements

Most people are familiar with Nokia because it is the leading seller of mobile phones in this country. It wasn't always so, as illustrated by this brief history:

1865   Nokia was established as a forest-enterprise business.
1898   Foundation of the Finnish Rubber Works.
1912   Establishment of Finnish Cable Works.
1967   Nokia, Finnish Rubber Works and Finnish Cable works merge to form Nokia Corporation.
1979   Nokia Mobile Phones, owned jointly by Nokia and Televa, was founded.
1982   Nokia introduced the first fully digitalised local exchange in Europe.
1991   The world's first genuine Global System for Mobile Communications call was made in Finland with equipment supplied by Nokia.
Today Nokia is the leading supplier of mobile phones to the UK market and is a global telecommunications supplier.

It was a natural step for Nokia to move into telecommunications. Its core skills in rubber and cable created the foundations for communications networks and to build telephone exchanges, before eventually moving on to the global development of mobile phones.

In the early 1990s, Nokia made a major shift in its activities by becoming a focused telecommunications company, as illustrated in the opposite chart.

Nokia had effectively decided that the future lay in:

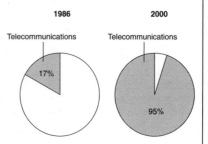

- Telecommunications products.
- The global rather than simply the national market.

Nokia's current strategy is based on:

- Reputation – customers and business partners associate Nokia with the leading edge in telecommunications provision.
- Profitability – as a growing business Nokia is able to plough back profits into developing its resources and capabilities.
- Resources and capabilities – over time Nokia has been able to develop an advanced set of resources (capital and equipment, intelligent employees, etc.) which enables it to drive forward in the global telecommunications business.
- Culture – Nokia has developed a pattern of working based on trying out new ideas and encouraging employees to make decisions rather than wait to be told what to do.

activity requires the co-operation and co-ordination of teams of resources.

- The **culture** (established ways of doing things in the organisation).

Much of an organisation's current **experience** (the accumulated knowledge and expertise that rests in the organisation) is based on its past achievements. Of course, in the modern world, this experience is by no means a guarantee of ongoing success. In a fast changing world, organisations often need to move their thinking forward rapidly rather than rely on the past. We see this, for example, in the way that in the post-Internet world major retailers have had to change their ways of thinking and operating to develop websites and other aspects of e-commerce.

The experience that an organisation builds up over time is not just about making goods and services. Just as importantly experience is concerned with a range of things that an organisation is good at – its **competences**. The **distinctive competences** of the organisation are the things that it does particularly well – e.g. market research, building good links with suppliers, guaranteeing quality at every stage of production, using state-of-the-art production processes, etc. A key part of examining the past achievements of an organisation therefore is to identify the distinctive competences which give a competitive advantage (Table 1).

For example, in the case of Manchester United the history of the club is associated with the glory days of great managers – the 'Busby Babes' of the 1950s – and more recently Alex Ferguson's teams in the late 1990s and early 2000s. The tradition of success has given the club a worldwide fan base and a heritage on which to build into the future. Today, the capabilities of the club are based on the huge cash surplus built up over the years, access to ongoing media and merchandising revenues, the ability to attract the best players in the world, etc.

Table 1 Examples of past achievement that organisations are able to build on in developing competitive advantage

Coca-Cola	Consumer focused marketing which has associated the brand with exciting lifestyles
Marks & Spencer	Strong links with other companies that are part of its supply chain (i.e. steps in the process of bringing goods to M&S)
Manchester United	Most successful British football club of all time in winning cup, league, and international trophies

Robert E. Grant argues that in the highly unstable business environment of today it makes sense to define a business in terms of 'what it is capable of doing'. The existing **capability** of a business depends heavily on what it has achieved in the past. Using capability as an organising framework, Grant has built a model for the creation of strategy based on a five-stage procedure. This starts from analysing the firm's resource base; appraising the firm's capabilities; analysing the profit earning potential of the firm's resources and capabilities; selecting a strategy; and extending and upgrading the firm's pool or resources and capabilities, as illustrated in Fig. 4.

In the case of a club like Manchester United, the firm's resources are not only based in its playing staff, but in everyone involved with the club, its stadium, its financial resources, and many other resources.

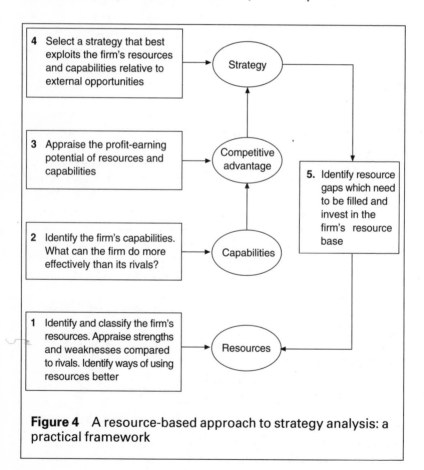

Figure 4 A resource-based approach to strategy analysis: a practical framework

Manchester United's capabilities lie in being able to play attractive, winning football better than any of its rivals. These capabilities can then be translated into profit-earning potential, e.g. through the ability to sell shirts with players' names on them across the globe. The strategy that the club has chosen is to dominate European and international club football by creating the best team in the world. Every now and then, new players are bought where gaps are identified in their existing resource base.

The firm's ability to sustain its competitive advantage over time depends upon the speed with which other firms can imitate its strategy. Imitation requires that a competitor overcomes two problems. First is the information problem: what is the competitive advantage of the successful rival, and how is it being achieved? Second is the strategy duplication problem: how can the would-be competitor amass the resources and capabilities required to imitate the successful strategy of the rival?

KEY WORDS

Reputation	Culture
Profitability	Experience
Resources	Competences
Capabilities	Distinctive competences

Further reading

Grant, R.M., in Segal-Horn, S. (ed.), Chapter 9, *The Strategy Reader*, Blackwell Business, Open University, 2001.

Johnson, G. and Scholes, K., *Exploring Corporate Strategy*, sixth edition, Chapter 4, Financial Times/Prentice Hall, 2001.

Lynch, R., *Corporate Strategy*, Chapter 1, Pitman Publishing, second edition, 2000.

Pearson, G., *Strategy in Action*, Chapter 1, Financial Times/Prentice Hall, 1999.

Further references

'Why is Manchester United So Successful?', S. Szymanski, *Business Strategy Review*, 1998, Volume 9 Issue 4, pp. 47-54.

Useful websites

Coca-Cola Website: http://www.cocacola.com/gateway.html

Manchester United Website: http://www.manutd.com/

Essay topics

1. Using examples show how organisations can develop the resources and distinctive competences over time which enable them to build ongoing successful strategies. [20 marks]
2. The success of an organisation's strategy is based as much on its past as on its future strategies. Discuss. [20 marks]

Data response – The ongoing success of Manchester United

Manchester United resembles brands like Coca-Cola, Marlboro cigarettes or Nescafé. Although they compete in markets crowded with superficially similar products, consumers have a strong tendency to rely on their established brand image in preference to their rivals. There are any number of cola drinks or cigarette brands in the world: indeed, in a blind taste test, consumers may be unable to distinguish a cola drink from genuine Coca-Cola, or Marlboro tobacco from any other brand. But the established brand names can still sell at higher prices than rivals and continue to dominate the market. In a sense, this is what Manchester United achieved: despite a lower level of League performance (in the period 1972-1990) than most of its major rivals, it was still able to attract more customers than these clubs.

It is quite rational for consumers to make choices based on brand image, even if they pay higher prices for the same product. First, choosing a brand name is generally simpler than choosing from a range of similar products in a world where it is costly to acquire information. If consumers had adequate information, they might choose to buy a better-valued brand of coffee each week, or choose to see a different football match. However, information processing is very costly: so it makes sense to go and see a team with an established track record. Few clubs in post-war England have had a better track record than Manchester United, even if this argument was beginning to wear a bit thin by the early 1990s.

Second, choosing a brand name is often a safer decision than gambling on a less well-known alternative choice. Brand names represent a long history of product development and promotion. The owners of a strong brand have a big incentive to try to maintain that image, while owners of products without such an image have less to worry about if they let the customer down. In that sense, just as Nescafé will always be committed to maintaining the quality of its coffee, Manchester United will always be committed to attractive match-winning football: to stop doing so would be to throw away a valuable image built up over many years. To fans considering the choice of club to support over a lifetime, this is a comforting thought.

Third, given that many people choose to support their local team, people who choose a non-local team are to some extent exceptional, and are clearly making a choice based on different criteria. One criterion for such a choice is likely to be history and image.

Finally, given that for most supporters there is usually a fairly large number of local teams to choose from, the actual choice of club can be a fairly random

> decision based on experiences early in one's youth. A decision such as this is likely to be influenced by the most popular team around at any point in time. To some extent, Manchester United is well supported because it has always been well supported.
>
> *Source*: Stefan Szymanski, *Business Strategy Review*, 1998

1. Why according to this article has Manchester United been able to maintain its fan base as a result of its past achievements? [4 marks]
2. How is the past achievement of Manchester United likely to influence the determination of its ongoing strategy? [6 marks]
3. Is it possible to draw parallels between the relationship of Manchester United's history and ongoing strategy with other organisations such as Nestlé and Coca-Cola? [10 marks]

Chapter Three

Scanning the environment

'The subject of strategy analyses the firm's relationships with its environment, and a business-strategy is a scheme for handling these relationships'. John Kay

Businesses are **decision making units** which develop strategies within an environment of change. The term 'environment' is used to describe the general conditions that surround an organisation – e.g. a competitive environment is one in which there is a lot of rivalry between firms, a dynamic environment is one in which there is rapid change, etc. In relation to the study of corporate strategy, the term 'the environment' is used to describe everything and everyone outside the organisation. Corporate strategists regard the environment as uncertain. The **business environment** is made up of a number of change elements as shown in Fig. 5.

Organisations need to be in tune with their environment. They therefore need to scan the environment continually to identify changes, in order to make appropriate strategic responses to these changes. Environmental auditing enables the organisation to be **proactive** (to shape change) rather than **reactive** (to respond to change). The effective

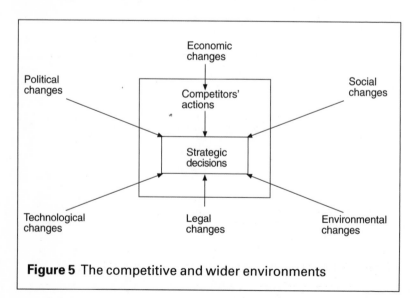

Figure 5 The competitive and wider environments

organisation will put a lot of effort into the process of **environmental auditing** and **scanning**.

There are three key steps in analysing the environment in which the organisation operates:

- Audit environmental influences. This involves identifying those environmental influences which have affected the organisation's development and performance in the past and seeking to identify those that will be significant in the future.
- Getting a view of how **stable** or **unstable** the environment is in which the organisation is operating. In a stable environment a **historical** and **present analysis** will be very useful. In an unstable environment a **future analysis** will be more relevant.
- Carrying out an analysis of specific environmental influences. A **structural analysis** (i.e. an analysis of the major factors and how these factors work together) will help to identify the key forces at work.

The principal tools for carrying out an environmental analysis are:

- The **PESTLE analysis**.
- **Scenario analysis**.
- **Auditing the market** – through **competitor analysis, strategic group analysis,** and **market segmentation**.
- The **SWOT analysis** (examined in Chapter 4).

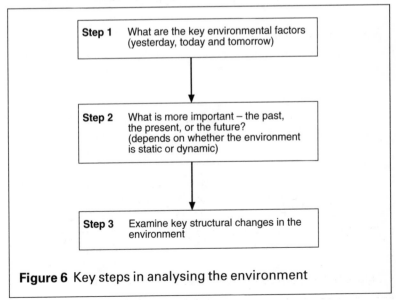

Figure 6 Key steps in analysing the environment

The PESTLE analysis

A PESTLE analysis looks at **political, economic, social, technological, legal** and **environmental changes** which are likely to affect the business. A PESTLE analysis is a very detailed study of these changes using a range of published sources such as government surveys, statistics about the state of the economy, social trend surveys, etc.

Political changes

A shift in political thinking associated with a change in government can have a major impact on business. For example, the Conservative Government of 1979-97 emphasised the importance of individuals in society looking after themselves and promoted an enterprise culture which encouraged business initiative. While the current Labour Government is still very concerned with the development of enterprise and partnership with business, it is also concerned with creating an 'inclusive society' in which the state seeks to include everyone rather than to exclude – e.g. through job creation schemes so that everyone is included in work in the economy. Under Labour, taxes on business have increased and measures such as the adoption of the minimum wage are seen by some businesses as harmful because it may raise their costs. Other political changes of significance are different parties views on the European Union. For example, Labour is far more committed to the UK adopting the euro at some stage in the future than is the Conservative leadership.

Economic changes

The economy goes through a cycle of periods of increasing economic activity followed by periods of recession. Business needs to be aware of where the economy stands in relation to this cycle. Boom periods encourage business strategies of expansion and growth while recessions create a hostile environment. Other economic factors that business needs to take into account are changes in interest rates and changes in exchange rates. A rise in interest rates discourages business growth, while reductions in interest rates have the reverse effect. A rise in the price of the £ against competing currencies may have a negative impact on businesses that export because this raises UK prices relative to those of competing firms. A reduction in the £ makes UK goods more competitive. Other key economic indicators that need to be considered in a PESTLE analysis include inflation, consumer expenditure and disposable income, and various costs (transport, energy, communication and raw material costs).

Social changes
Over time many changes take place in society which are relevant to business. Key changes include those in population, in tastes and buying patterns, in employment patterns, etc. For example, an ageing population will benefit businesses whose customer base is made up of older people. Trends and tastes are constantly changing leading to regular changes in buying patterns. Employment patterns also need to be studied – for example the growing numbers of women in the workplace have led to an increased demand for convenience food, etc. Other important social changes are shifts in values and culture, education and health, and distribution of income.

Technological changes
The application of information and communications technologies in the first decade of the twenty-first century is having a dramatic impact on business. More people than ever before are buying online, forcing most large businesses to develop strategies involving e-commerce. Other technological changes involve the product of new research initiatives, and levels of expenditure on research and development, and government support of new technologies.

Legal changes
Organisations need to anticipate and prepare themselves for changes in the law. For example, in recent years many organisations have been able to anticipate tighter legislation with regards to Health and Safety standards enabling organisations to bring in the required changes well in advance of legal requirements.

Environmental change
Increasingly, organisations have had to develop environmental strategies. Today there are International and British Standards for environmental quality procedures. Organisations need to be in the forefront of making these changes rather than come from a catch-up position. In addition, organisations need to respond to 'green issues' being voiced by customers and community groups.

A good PESTLE analysis is not simply a list of changes in the environment that may affect the business, rather it involves identifying the key structural changes in the business environment that are relevant to a specific business, and the links that exist between these changes. The PESTLE analysis enables the organisation to create the strategies that prepare it for change in advance of the changes occurring.

Forecasting the environment

There are a number of important steps involved in analysing the environment. The most important of these are:

- To identify which forces are the most important and why they are so significant.
- To forecast how these forces might change in the future.
- To build expectations and predictions into decision making.

Scenario analysis

Another approach to coping with a changing environment is through scenario analysis. This approach was pioneered by the oil company Shell in the 1970s. At the time, Shell was all too aware of how its industry could rapidly change as the result of oil producers joining together to push up the price of oil.

What Shell did was to devise a series of scenarios. A scenario is a model of a future environment for the organisation. The organisation can then plan strategies to deal with a range of scenarios. For example, Shell could plan scenarios for a rise in the price of oil by 50 per cent over the next ten years, or a 10 per cent rise etc. Scenarios could involve wars in significant parts of the world, or the complete banning of private cars on the roads as a result of 'green pressure'. The aim of scenario planning is not to predict the future but to explore a set of possibilities and then to prepare appropriate responses.

Richard Lynch sets out the following guidance for building scenarios:

- Start from an **unusual viewpoint**. Examples might include the stance of a major competitor, a radical change of government or the outbreak of war.
- Develop a **qualitative description** of a group of possible events or a **narrative** that shows how events will unfold.
- Explore the **outcomes** of this description or narrative of events by building two or three scenarios of what might happen. Two scenarios will lend themselves to a 'most optimistic outcome' and a 'worst possible outcome'.
- Include the inevitable **uncertainty** in each scenario and explore the consequences of this uncertainty to the organisation concerned. PESTLE factors should provide some clues here.
- Test the **usefulness** of the scenario by the extent to which it leads to new strategic thinking rather than merely the continuance of existing strategy.

Competitor analysis

There are two contrasting views about how best to deal with competitors. One view is that an understanding of your competitors, their actions, and how to beat them is at the heart of competitive advantage. The other view is that you focus on your own business, identify your own core competences, concentrate on doing them really well, cut down your costs, identify and satisfy your customers and forget about the competition.

The best way forward probably lies somewhere between these two views. There is no point in studying competitors just because it seems like the right thing to do. In studying competitors you need to have some fairly focused questions which are of use to your own development. Michael Porter argues that effective strategic management is the positioning of an organisation, relative to its competitors, in such a way that it outperforms them. Organisations therefore need to know something about the competitors that they wish to outperform.

Michael Porter argues that **five forces** determine the profitability of an industry (Fig. 7).

At the centre of the industry are **rivals** and their competitive strategies linked to, for example, pricing or promotional activity. However, it is also important to look beyond one's immediate competitors as there are other determinants of profitability in the industry.

In particular, there might be competition from **substitute products or services,** these alternatives may be seen as substitutes by buyers even though they are part of a different industry. An example would be plastic bottles, cans and foil for packaging soup. Or, there may also be a potential

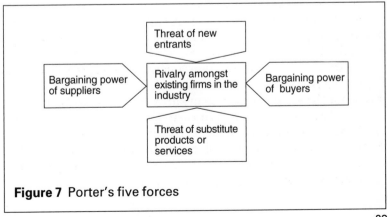

Figure 7 Porter's five forces

threat of new entrants, for example new firms might move into producing packaging materials if the profits are sufficiently attractive. Finally, it is important to appreciate that companies purchase from **suppliers** and sell to **buyers**. If these forces are powerful they are in a position to bargain profits away through reduced margins, by forcing either cost increases or price decreases. For example, for many years Marks & Spencer has had considerable power in forging supply contracts with suppliers of textiles and foodstuffs because it is such a large buyer.

Any company must seek to understand the nature of its competitive environment if it is to be successful in achieving its objectives and in establishing appropriate strategies. If a company fully understands the nature of the five forces, and particularly appreciates which ones are the most important, it will be in a stronger position to defend itself against any threats, and to influence the forces with its strategy. The situation, of course, is subject to continual change, and the nature and relative power of the forces will change, resulting in the need to monitor and stay aware which is continuous. Hence the importance of 'scanning the environment'.

Strategic group analysis

The boundaries of an 'industry' are not always clear. Firms may compete closely with each other although they may not appear to be in the same industry (e.g. producers of magazines for teenagers and suppliers of pop videos) – while firms that are in the same industry may not necessarily be close competitors (e.g. suppliers of newspapers aimed at different target audiences).

Another way of looking at competition is that of **strategic group analysis** which seeks to identify organisations that are following similar strategies of competing in similar ways. Such groups can be identified because they have two or three sets of key characteristics which form the basis of competition. For example, in the European food marketing industry it is possible to identify a number of strategic groups – e.g. multinational major brands such as Nestlé and Unilever. These multinational major branders share common characteristics of having a wide geographical coverage in nearly every country in the European Union, and at the same time having a very high marketing intensity (measured by costs as a per cent of sales). In the same industry there are other strategic groups, e.g. national major branders (for example, UK manufacturers focusing on the UK market alone with a high marketing intensity), and minor national branders (for example, UK manufacturers focusing on the UK market alone with a low marketing intensity).

Adidas reports sharp nine-month profit fall

Adidas, the world's second-largest sportswear and equipment maker, yesterday reported a sharp drop in nine-month profits, but offered investors some positive news by forecasting an improvement in its performance in the US market by the middle of 2001.

Net profit in the January-September period fell 22 per cent to €177m ($150m), while sales rose 7 per cent to €4.4bn. Adidas had forecast a 20 per cent decline in net profits in 2000.

Investors and analysts have become highly sensitive to Adidas' deteriorating performance in the US, the world's largest sporting goods and sportswear market, since it has become the group's Achilles heel.

After failing to update its once-trendy product line and losing market share to arch-rival Nike, the group has seen further competition from clothing designers such as Tommy Hilfiger and Ralph Lauren.

Adidas said sales of its Salomon and TaylorMade Golf brands should see double-digit growth in 2000 and compensate for weakness in North America and negative currency effects.

The group also said it had accomplished most of its restructuring programme, which will eventually lead to annual savings of DM100m (€51m, $43m) and boost the company's overall efficiency.

Analysts were particularly surprised when Adidas confirmed its goal to boost net profits by 15 per cent annually starting in 2001 in spite of negative currency effects.

Adidas has suffered from the strong dollar because it sources most of its products in Asia, where it pays for them in dollars, but generates more than half of its sales in Europe.

'The year 2000 has been a year of transition to prepare for healthy top and bottom line growth starting in 2001,' said Herbert Hainer, chief operating officer, who is slated to succeed Robert Louis-Dreyfuss as chairman when he retires early next year.

Adidas also said it would boost its US market share in the apparel and footwear sector to 20 per cent from its current 12 per cent.

Nike, which is twice as big as Adidas, has a market share of 40 per cent in the US. In Europe, Adidas and Nike maintain a fierce battle for leadership with about 24 per cent market share each.

'Overall, the US situation is less worse than we had expected – for Adidas that is good news,' said Owe Weinreich at Bankfesellschaft Berlin.

Adidas' order backlog in the US continued to be negative, but it showed the first signs of improvement.

Adidas shares rose 3.9 per cent to close at €56.10. Adidas has seen its shares fall 40 per cent since the beginning of the year after underperforming the market throughout 1999.

Financial Times, 3 November 2000, by Uta Harnischfeger

Strategic group analysis is helpful to an organisation in identifying direct competitors, and also in identifying gaps in the market.

Organisations like Adidas, the sportswear and equipment maker have to keep a close eye on their competitive environment. In terms of strategic group analysis, Adidas can be placed in a small group of multinational major branders which includes its much bigger rival Nike. The boxed news item on the previous page shows how, at the end of 2000, Adidas had been suffering from poor performance in the United States because of falling competitiveness of many of its products, strong competition from Nike – as well as the high price of the dollar.

Market segmentation analysis

Where specific groups of customers with broadly similar needs can be identified and targeted they are known as **market segments**, and products and services can be differentiated to meet the needs of these segments. Customers and users have different characteristics and needs, and behave in different ways. Identifying which organisations are competing in different market segments enables the organisation to better understand its competitive position.

Managing the environment

PESTLE, scenario analysis and competitor analysis, should enable the organisation to understand how dynamic and how complex the environment is in which it is operating. The organisation needs to be **proactive** rather than **reactive** in managing its environment. In other words it should make change rather than respond to change.

Strategic managers need to have a good understanding of the key structural forces that influence their organisation and the relative strengths of key stakeholders in influencing change. The organisation will never be able to predict every change in its environment but by careful scanning it should be able to keep ahead of competitors.

KEY WORDS

Decision making units
Business environment
Proactive
Reactive
Environmental auditing
Scanning
Stable environment
Unstable environment
Historical analysis
Present analysis
Future analysis
Structural analysis
PESTLE analysis
Scenario analysis
Market audit
Competitor analysis
Market segmentation
SWOT analysis
Economic changes

Social changes
Technological changes
Legal changes
Environmental changes
Political changes
Unusual viewpoint
Qualitative description
Narrative
Outcomes
Uncertainty
Usefulness
Five forces
Rivalry
Substitute products or services
Bargaining power of suppliers
Bargaining power of buyers
Strategic group analysis
Market segments

Further reading

Greenley, G.E., Chapters 3 and 4, *Strategic Management*, Prentice Hall, 1999.

Johnson, G. and Scholes, K., Chapter 3, *Exploring Corporate Strategy*, Financial Times/Prentice Hall, sixth edition, 2000.

Napuk, K., Chapter 2, *The Strategy Led Business*, McGraw-Hill, third edition, 2000.

Thompson, J.L., Chapter 1, *Strategy in Action*, Chapman and Hall, 1995.

Useful websites

Adidas website: www.adidas.com
Shell website: www.shell.com

Essay Topics

1. (a) Explain how a PESTLE analysis will help an organisation to deal with a dynamic environment. [8 marks]

(b) What economic and social factors would be particularly important in the environmental analysis of a multinational European company producing confectionery? [12 marks]

2. (a) How can a five forces analysis help an organisation to develop a picture of the competitive environment in which it is operating? [10 marks]

(b) Describe one other approach that a large European multinational company could use to assess the nature of the competition that it is facing. [10 marks]

Data Response – Shell's profits soar on oil prices

In November 2000 Royal Dutch/Shell, the Anglo-Dutch energy group, reported an 80 per cent jump in its third quarter earnings to a record $3.25bn (£2.24bn) thanks to the 'exceptional oil prices' during the period.

Average Brent oil prices for the quarter of $30.45 a barrel helped boost net profits by 29 per cent to $3.06bn, while net profits for the first nine months were up 60 per cent to $9.6bn.

Sir Mark Moody-Stuart, Shell's chairman, defended the results as 'exceptional'. But he noted '… these high prices have meant exceptionally difficult retail markets for our customers and for ourselves'.

Sir Mark pointedly warned of 'leaner periods in future', but noted that Shell had made steady progress on leading performance indicators. These include a 16.6 per cent return on average capital employed over the year to the end of September against 2.9 per cent a year ago, and oil and natural gas volume growth of 6 per cent and 8 per cent, respectively, in the year up to November. The infusion of cash left Shell with a debt ratio of just 12.4 per cent and a cash balance of almost $8bn, a fact that helped fuel expectations that it might be in the market for an acquisition. Attention focused on Shell's possible interest in downstream refining and marketing assets that were likely to be sold in the US following the proposed merger of Chevron and Texaco.

1. Explain how changes in the economic environment which were outside of Shell's control enabled it to develop new elements to its strategy? [10 marks]

2. How might Shell use scenario planning to prepare itself for 'leaner periods in future'? [10 marks]

Chapter Four

Assessing corporate strengths and weaknesses and identifying opportunities and threats

'The best way to declare confidently a future direction that sustains commitment and belief is to conduct a realistic and detailed assessment of your strengths and weaknesses. This exercise is usually described by the acronym of SWOT, standing for the first letters of the words Strengths, Weaknesses, Opportunities and Threats. Another name for the exercise is WOTS-UP: weaknesses, opportunities, threats and strengths.' Kerry Napuk

Scanning the environment involves the monitoring, evaluating and communication of information about the environment to key people within the organisation. Environmental scanning is carried out to identify **strategic factors** – which are external or internal to the organisation and which will determine the future of the business. The simplest way to scan the environment is through SWOT analysis.

SWOT is an acronym used to describe the particular Strengths, Weaknesses, Opportunities and Threats that are strategic factors for a specific business (Fig. 8). The student is likely to come across SWOT analysis in studying marketing in relation to the preparation of

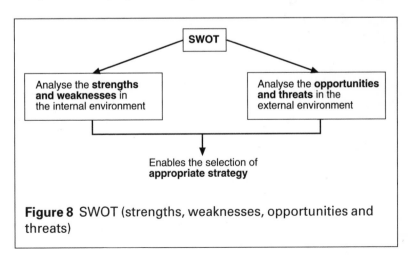

Figure 8 SWOT (strengths, weaknesses, opportunities and threats)

marketing strategies. In this book we are concerned with the use of the SWOT analysis for the development of corporate (whole organisation) strategies.

Strengths and **weaknesses** are internal to the organisation and often relate to resources – e.g. the organisation does not have people with the right skills (a weakness), the organisation is generating a healthy profit (a strength), etc.

Opportunities and **threats** relate to the external environment, for example the threat of a downturn in the economy, or the opportunity of new markets abroad. Opportunities often relate to the development of new customers and new markets, and threats often relate to the actions of competitors.

Carrying out an effective SWOT analysis enables an organisation to develop strategies for the future. Having carried out a detailed SWOT the following questions should be asked:

- How can we reduce or neutralise critical weaknesses or turn them into strengths?
- How can we reduce or neutralise critical threats or even turn them into opportunities?
- How can we best exploit our strengths in relation to our opportunities?
- What new markets and market segments might be suitable for our existing strengths and capabilities?
- Given the changes that are taking place in our existing markets, what changes do we need to make to products, services and processes?

For example, the organisation that recognises that it has a weakness in terms of not having the right people with the right skills can engage in a training programme to make sure that its people are ahead of the field, or recruit new people with the right skills. The organisation that recognises the threat that its competitors are gaining an edge by employing sophisticated e-commerce techniques can develop its own website and e-commerce presence.

Getting the internal environment right

We have already seen that key areas of strength for an organisation involve having the right resources to match desired strategies. It is important to carry out an **audit of strategic resources** (e.g. financial resources, human resources, information systems, plant, etc.) to make sure that they are being managed well. The value of resources depends on how they are being managed, controlled and used. In addition, the

Carrying out a SWOT analysis at LINK in 2000

Today, cash machines or ATMs (automated teller machines) are the most popular method of withdrawing cash for most personal customers.

The UK's ATMs are linked together through the LINK network. LINK is a system joining together the UK's major financial institutions (banks and building societies).

LINK is owned by 22 of these institutions. In the modern world in which customers dominate the way in which services are provided, it is essential that an account holder in any bank or building society is able to access their money at the most convenient location. The creation of LINK means that a Barclays account holder is able to withdraw cash from an ATM belonging to any one of the other 38 members of LINK.

ATMs are not just cash dispensers, they also provide a range of other banking services such as providing balance enquiries.

LINK is now at a crossroads in terms of its ongoing development. Today, it has little direct competition in providing a network for ATMs. As a result, it is in the envious position of having a core product which serves as a cash cow enabling healthy profits to be made. However, it needs to look to the long term. The organisation that stands still will frequently be overtaken. LINK therefore needs to build a strategy to use its profits in a way that will secure its future.

To get a clear idea of where it wants to go in the future LINK has carried out a SWOT analysis.

The SWOT analysis revealed these key strengths:

- LINK is a low-cost, high-quality processor.
- It is a stable company – its key business activity serving as a cash cow.
- It has market dominance.
- It has a quality team of people working for it.
- The owners are the customers.

Examples of internal weaknesses included the narrowness of the market that it was operating in, and the lack of any clear vision as to how to take the organisation forward.

Threats identified as facing the organisation included:

- The development of substitutes for cash.
- The trend towards globalisation of markets.
- The possible growth of competitors in the payment systems market.

At the same time a number of key opportunities were identified:

- The rapid growth of e-commerce.
- The growth of new payment types.
- The rapid development of Switch as a means of making payments.
- Geographic expansion into Europe and beyond.

(cont'd overleaf)

Having carried out this SWOT analysis, LINK was able to create a strategy for the future. A strategy is a plan of action as to how an organisation will move forward. Given LINK's position in 2000 as a highly profitable organisation with resources that could be ploughed into future development, the new strategy contained the following elements. Firstly, it is seeking to mushroom outwards from its core activity as 'ATM UK'. LINK is therefore developing a range of new payment systems which take into account all the new ways in which people make payments in the UK including switching arrangements. LINK's strategy also involves geographical expansion through the creation of joint ventures and partnership arrangements with overseas providers. Through the use of digital and other modern technologies LINK is planning to provide a total customer service which will take account of all of the new ways in which customers deal with their banks, e.g. through remote interactions involving the internet, interactive digital TV and voice telephone.

LINK could have rested on its laurels as 'ATM UK'. However, if it had done so it would have been signing its own death warrant. The SWOT analysis revealed that in the world of rapidly advancing technology there is always a competitor out there with the capability to develop more advanced technologies which will capture tomorrow's marketplace.

organisation needs to make sure that it has the right structure and culture to make the strategies work. The **structure** of the organisation is the way in which the organisation is organised. Today, organisations are seeking the sorts of structures that enable flexibility (i.e. the ability to respond to change). The **culture** of an organisation is the typical way of doing things in an organisation based on a collection of beliefs, expectations and values that have developed over time. Building a strong organisation therefore is not just about building a collection of the right resources, it also involves developing the structures and the ways of doing things in the organisation that will ensure best use of those resources.

Creating the right match with the external environment

In the previous chapter, we saw that organisations need to understand the wider environment in which they operate. In addition, the organisation needs to be in tune with its external stakeholders (the **stakeholder environment**) (Fig. 9).

Stakeholders are those individuals and groups who depend on an organisation to achieve some of their goals and on whom in turn the organisation depends for the full realisation of its goals.

Stakeholders are individuals and groups which are involved with the organisation in some way and include shareholders, suppliers, governments, employees/trade unions, special interest groups, competitors, customers, creditors, trade associations and communities.

In creating a strategy it is important to take into account the wishes of these stakeholders and the coalitions that exist between these stakeholder groupings.

Shareholders are often the most important stakeholder. Their prime interest will be in receiving a good return on their investment, and they may therefore seek to block strategies which threaten the dividends that they expect to receive. However, in given situations other stakeholders may be more significant – for example, the government may block a business strategy to merge with another company because of the resulting monopoly situation that might arise. Employees and trade unions may resist strategies which threaten employment. Customers are always an important stakeholder interest and no company can afford to alienate its customers.

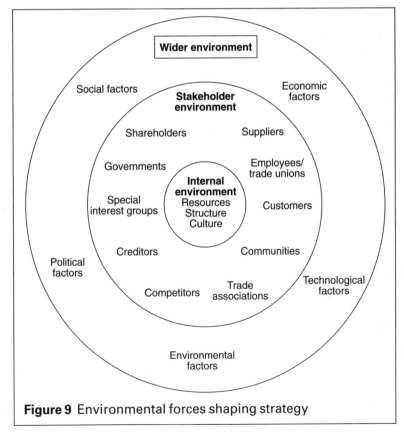

Figure 9 Environmental forces shaping strategy

		Level of interest	
		Low	High
Power	Low	A Minimal effort	B Keep informed
	High	C Keep satisfied	D Key player

Figure 10 The power/interest matrix

The interests and power of stakeholder groupings play an important part in the selection of a strategy. The **power/interest matrix** shown in Fig. 10 outlines a way of evaluating the effect of stakeholders and of drawing conclusions about the way they should be treated.

Stakeholders with little interest and little power are not significant players and need not have much attention given to them. Stakeholders with high interest and much power, however, need to be considered much more carefully.

E-V-R Congruence

David Marshall chose the **E-V-R Congruence** framework to demonstrate the underlying concept of strategic management (Fig. 11). Strategies are being managed effectively when the organisation's resources are used in such a way that the business meets the demands and expectations of its stakeholders, and responds and adapts to changes in the environment. In other words, it has strengths which take advantage of the opportunities and deal with potential threats in an environment of change.

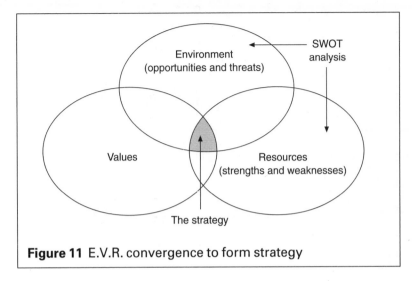

Figure 11 E.V.R. convergence to form strategy

E   Managers would need to fully understand the dynamics, opportunities and threats present in their competitive **environment,** and that they are paying full regard to the wider **environment.**

V   The **values** of the organisation would need to match the needs of the environment and the key success factors. These values would need to be shared and followed throughout the organisation.

R   The **resources** of the organisation would need to be managed strategically taking into account the strengths, weaknesses and opportunities for the organisation.

The first four chapters of this book have shown how preparing effective strategies is all about creating a match between an organisation's **capabilities** (what it is able to do) and the environmental conditions in which it operates. The organisation needs to identify carefully its key areas of **competence** (what it does particularly well), and the strategic resources that are available to it. These capabilities then need to be matched to the environment and to the opportunities and risks that exist in the environment. Of course, the organisation will need to think of how it can extend its capabilities to best meet the challenges in its changing environment (Fig. 12).

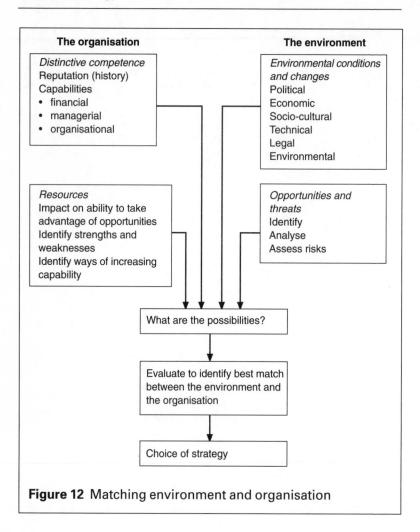

Figure 12 Matching environment and organisation

```
┌─────────────────────────────────────────────────────┐
│                      KEY WORDS                        │
│  Strategic factors          Shareholders              │
│  SWOT                       Wider environment         │
│  Strengths                  Internal environment      │
│  Weaknesses                 External environment      │
│  Opportunities              Power/interest matrix     │
│  Threats                    E-V-R congruence          │
│  Audit of strategic resources  Environment            │
│  Structure                  Values                    │
│  Culture                    Resources                 │
│  Stakeholder environment    Capabilities              │
│  Stakeholders               Competence                │
└─────────────────────────────────────────────────────┘
```

Further reading

Napuk, K., Chapter 3, *The Strategy Led Business*, McGraw-Hill, third edition, 2000.

Pearson, G., Chapter 5, *Strategy in Action*, Financial Times/Prentice Hall, 1999.

Wheelen, T. and Hunger, J., *Strategic Management and Business Policy*, Addison Wesley, 2000.

Thompson, J., Chapter 8, *Strategic Management*, Chapman Hall, fourth edition, 2000.

Useful website

LINK website: www.link.co.uk

Essay topics

1. What is a SWOT analysis? How can a well-constructed SWOT analysis enable an organisation to develop an effective corporate strategy?   [20 marks]

2. (a) What part should stakeholders play in the creation of an organisational strategy?   [8 marks]

   (b) How might stakeholder interest clash? How should organisations reconcile these differing interests in the creation of a strategy?   [12 marks]

Data response question – Stakeholder interests at Firestone

In August 2000 the well-known American tyre producer Firestone (owned by Bridgestone of Japan) was rocked by news that the US government (National Highway Traffic Administration) was demanding a massive recall of tyres. The recall of up to 10 million tyres was as a result of a government probe into the company to determine whether faulty tyres might have been responsible for some 88 deaths across America and another 250 injuries. The probe indicated that the tyres had flaws that could cause tread to peel away and lead to blow-outs.

The impact of the probe was to lead to a large-scale downward revision in profit forecasts for the company and the alienation of consumers such as the Ford motor company which fitted a number of vehicles with Firestone tyres.

The crisis could not have happened at a worse time for the company which was under threat of union strike action at factories all across the USA as a result of declining job security, and a deterioration of pay and conditions.

1. Who do you see as being the main stakeholders in Firestone; explain the stake of each of the groupings. [4 marks]
2. Which of these stakeholder groupings would in normal circumstances have most power in shaping the strategy of Firestone? [2 marks]
3. How might the events described in the case study have shifted the relative power of stakeholders in Firestone? [4 marks]
4. What actions do strategic managers need to take to turn weaknesses and threats into strengths and opportunities?
[10 marks]

Chapter Five

Choosing a direction for the organisation

'A corporate mission statement is useful for providing direction and guidance.

Ideally the mission will state the basic purpose of the business, together with a summary of appropriate activities, how progress towards achievement of the purpose might be managed and monitored and how the company might create competitive advantage.

It should be relevant for all the stakeholders, and also be understood and supported by all the company's employees.' John L. Thompson

Strategic managers establish the **purposes** and **objectives** for an organisation to work towards and then choose and **implement** (put into practice) the strategies that will enable the organisation to meet these purposes and objectives.

The mission

All organisations should have a purpose which they seek to work towards. Today, it is common practice for organisations to set out this purpose in a **mission** for the organisation. A simple definition of a mission is 'The essential purpose of the organization ... the nature of the business(es) it is in and the customers it seeks to serve and satisfy.'

For example, Newcastle United PLC set out their mission in the following way:

> 'The business of Newcastle United is football – our aim is to play attractive football, to win trophies, to satisfy our supporters and shareholders and to continually improve our position as a top European club'.

This **mission statement** encapsulates the aims and purposes of the club. It then becomes possible for everyone in the club to focus on strategies devised to achieve the mission (see Table 2).

A quality mission statement will define the fundamental, **unique purpose** that sets the company apart from other firms of its type and identifies the **scope** of the company's operations in terms of goods and services offered and markets served. It might also include the firm's **philosophy** about how it does business and treats its employees. For example, the charity Oxfam sets out its mission as:

'Oxfam works with others to overcome "poverty" and "suffering".'

Table 2 The mission statement of Newcastle United PLC analysed

Aspect of mission	Supporting strategy
Play attractive football	Appoint a management team capable of delivering attractive football
Win trophies	Build the team and support structures that will ensure competitive success
Satisfy supporters	Win success and give value for money
Satisfy shareholders	Win large supporter base who also purchase club merchandise
Improve European position	Generate the success that will support a European strategy, e.g. purchase of world-class players

The mission needs to be realistic given the organisation's existing resources and capabilities and to provide a clear focus for organisational activity.

Having a 'sense of mission' is not the same thing as having a **'mission statement'** (a written statement outlining the mission). It is possible for an organisation to have a mission statement but only a poor sense of mission. A mission statement may simply be propaganda or wishful thinking on the part of management.

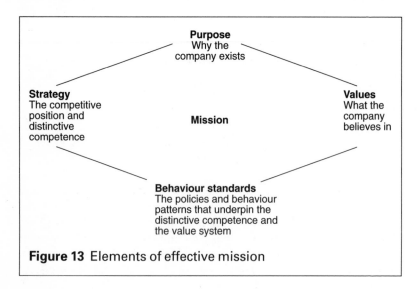

Figure 13 Elements of effective mission

Andrew Campbell and Sally Young of the Ashridge Management School have set out a model for an effective mission for an organisation based on four key elements (Fig. 13).

Mission and the culture of the organisation

The mission of an organisation should reflect and guide the **culture** of an organisation. The culture of the organisation is the typical pattern of behaviours, values and beliefs within an organisation. American textbooks sometimes simply define culture as 'the way we do things around here'. For example, some organisations are very rule bound with formal patterns of communication and set patterns and procedures. In contrast, other organisations are far more dynamic and democratic allowing people within the organisation to make decisions for themselves. Some organisations have **'backward facing cultures'** where patterns of behaviour are determined by what happened in the past, while others are far more concerned with the future.

Because the mission sets out the purpose of the organisation it should help to give a view of the culture of the organisation. Changing the mission of an organisation is likely to involve trying to change the culture of the organisation. This is not always easy because there are a number of barriers to change which are discussed in Chapter 9.

Objectives

Whilst the mission provides a purpose for the organisation it is also essential to establish **objectives** (or goals) to work towards.

Corporate (organisational) objectives provide the direction for strategic management, and relate to the performance of the total organisation. Corporate objectives can then be further translated down into **operational objectives** for operational decision making.

Definitions

Corporate objectives are ones which set goals for the whole organisation to work towards.

Operational objectives set goals for shorter-term decision making involving the key processes that the organisation is concerned with on a day-to-day basis.

Corporate strategy needs to be based on clear and decisive objectives. Efforts need to be directed towards clearly understood, decisive, and attainable overall goals. The overriding goals of the strategy for all units must remain clear enough to provide continuity

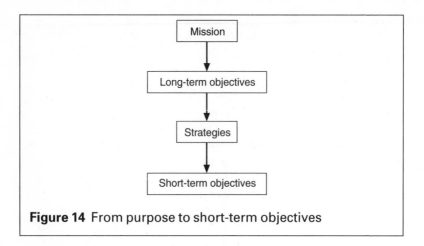

Figure 14 From purpose to short-term objectives

and cohesion for tactical choices during the time horizon of the strategy.

A distinction can be made between long-term objectives and short-term objectives.

Long-term objectives focus on the desired performance and results of the organisation on an on-going basis. **Short-term objectives** are concerned with near-term performance targets that the organisation is working towards in pursuing its strategies (Fig. 14).

A further distinction can be made between open and closed objectives. **Closed objectives** are clearly measurable and are often finance based – for example, to achieve a rate of return on capital employed in the business of 18 per cent over the next twelve months. In the previous chapter we saw that Ryanair had set itself some closed objectives in terms of expanding its capacity to 9 million passengers in 2001 and 14 million passengers by 2004.

Open objectives are less specific and set continuing goals for the organization, e.g. 'to ensure continued customer satisfaction' or 'to achieve a competitive return on capital employed'.

Management by objectives

In the 1960s Peter Drucker popularised the idea of **Management by Objectives (MbO)** and this approach is still popular with some managers today.

Management by objectives enables managers:

- to focus the management task on a specific outcome (e.g. a 5 per cent increase in sales;

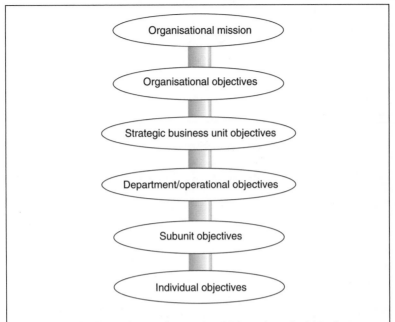

Figure 15 Drilling down through a hierarchy of objectives.
Strategic Business Units (SBU) are parts of the organisation
which are seen as distinct in planning strategies. For
example, a food company may be divided into a number of
food categories each of which comprises an SBU

- to provide a means of assessing whether the outcome has been
  achieved after the event (did sales increase by 5 per cent); and
- to set ongoing objectives (if the 5 per cent sales target was achieved
  should a new 6 per cent outcome be set for the next period).

The great thing about objectives is that they can be 'drilled down'
through the various levels within the organisation – enabling all
organisational activities to be geared towards achieving corporate
mission as shown in Fig. 15.

Drucker identifies a number of key result areas that it is possible to
establish organisation objectives for:

- market standing
- innovation
- productivity
- physical and financial resources

- profitability
- manager performance and development
- employee performance and attitude
- public responsibility.

Today, all organisations set objectives. However, in a dynamic business environment it is widely accepted that these objectives need to have flexibility built into them.

The characteristics of objectives

To be most helpful in achieving its mission objectives the organization needs to have a number of important characteristics: they need to be

- specific
- easily understood
- widely communicated
- challenging
- attainable
- measurable.

A **specific objective** is clear and precise. It gives direction, and it is then possible to check that the direction has been followed. In a football match, 'to get the ball forward' may not be a specific enough objective. To get the ball forward to the head of Heskey and the feet of Owen is a lot more specific. In selling, to get Mars Bars into every confectionery retailing outlet in England and Wales is a lot more specific than 'to get Mars products into more retail outlets'.

Objectives need to be **easily understood**. The managers that create objectives often only play a small part in the operationalisation of these objectives. Objectives need to be presented in clear and easy to understand language so that there is no ambiguity. For example, an objective 'to increase output' may lead to an increase in sub-standard products – when managers really mean 'to increase the level of output of items which meet the required quality standards'.

Objectives need to be **widely communicated**. Organisational objectives often involve everyone in the organisation. Serious deficiencies will occur if key objectives are not communicated widely to everyone concerned. For example, if the organisation places strong emphasis on objectives related to customer service – then everyone in the organisation has an internal or external customer. Communication of objectives needs to be closely tied up with training and development, and with communication channels in the organisation.

Objectives need to be **challenging**. Objectives should not be too easy to achieve. They should stretch the organisation, its business units and people in a rewarding way. If objectives are set at too low a level then they will not be taken seriously. People may take a minimalist approach to achieving these objectives. For example, in the 1970s British Leyland, a UK car manufacturer, had a reputation for establishing low standards. Some employees were able to quickly meet production targets and then sleep or play cards for the remainder of the night shift.

Objectives need to be **attainable**. Objectives should be capable of being met while at the same time not being too demanding. When objectives are unattainable this can lead to frustration, and loss of commitment. People may feel that they are being given impossible demands – and thus become demotivated. Indeed when they feel that the objectives set are a 'joke' they may deliberately set out to sabotage processes and activities.

Objectives need to be **measurable** wherever appropriate. Objectives can provide a quantifiable measure of where the organisation is going. By creating quantified objectives it becomes possible to answer questions such as:

- What do we need to do to meet the objectives?
- How far have we come in meeting objectives?
- Have we met objectives?
- What more needs to be done to meet the objectives? etc.

Organisational vision

Some organisations set out a **vision statement** as well as a mission statement. The vision sets out the company's vision of some future state that they are working towards. The vision statement helps the organisation to work towards this future state.

Richard Koch defines a vision as 'an inspiring view of what a company could become, a dream about its future shape and success, a picture of a potential future for a firm, a glimpse into its Promised Land. A vision is a long term aspiration of a leader for his or her firm, that can be described to colleagues and that will urge them on through the desert.'

There is thus a clear difference between mission and vision. Mission is why a firm exists, its purpose. Vision is a view of what the firm could become, imagining a desired future.

For example, the founders of Starbucks, a chain of coffee bars that originally started up in America in the 1970s and later came to Europe, had a vision of Starbucks as:

'the chosen "Third Place" for customers'

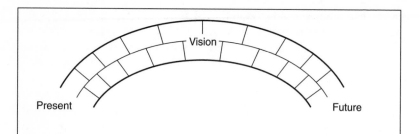

Figure 16 The vision is the bridge linking the present and the future

(the first and second places being the home and work). The vision therefore was to see the Starbucks coffee bar replace the old-fashioned 'bar' as the most popular leisure location.

The vision is thus the bridge which enables the organisation to make the transition between the present and the future (Fig. 16). For example, Nestlé which is widely recognised as the largest world food company has recently created for itself the vision of becoming recognised as 'The World Food Company' in the early part of the 21st century.

Organisational values

In addition to mission, objectives, and visions, many organisations also set out a series of **values** which will guide their actions. The values set out how the organisation will behave and how its people will behave.

For example, Nestlé has set out its values in terms of a series of characteristics which it describes as its corporate personality:

Confident	Trustworthy and trusting, responsible, ambitious, proud.
Empathetic	Open, respectful, responsive, genuine, full of integrity, decent.
Conscientious	Meticulous, courageous, scrupulous, concise, responsible, strong work ethic.
Practical	Pragmatic, straightforward, down to earth, uncomplicated.
Expert	Experienced, knowledgeable, professional.
Innovative	Dynamic, far sighted.

KEY WORDS

Purposes	Long-term objectives
Objectives	Short-term objectives
Implement	Closed objectives
Mission	Open objectives
Mission statement	Management by Objectives
Unique purpose	(MbO)
Scope	Strategic Business Units
Philosophy	Specific objectives
Values	Easily understood objectives
Behaviour standards	Widely communicated
Culture	objectives
Backward facing culture	Challenging objectives
Corporate/organisational	Attainable objectives
objectives	Measurable objectives
Operational objectives	Vision statement

Further reading

Greenley, G.E., Chapters 6 and 7, *Strategic Management*, Prentice Hall, 1999.

Napuk, K., Chapters 3 and 4, *The Strategy Led Business*, McGraw-Hill, third edition, 2000.

Needham, D., Dransfield, R., *et al*, Chapter 28, *Business for Higher Awards*, Heinemann, 2000.

Thompson, J.L., Chapter 5, *Strategic Management*, Thomson Business Press, fourth edition, 2000.

Additional references

Koch, R., *The Financial Times Guide to Strategy*, FT/Pitman Publishing, second edition, 2000.

Useful websites

Starbucks website: www.starbucks.com
Nestlé website: www.nestle.com

Essay topics

1. (a) Using examples explain how the mission and objectives of an organisation should provide the organisation with a clear sense of purpose and direction. [10 marks]

   (b) How might a series of closed objectives enable a retailing organisation to develop clear strategies? [10 marks]

2. In February 2001, Leicester City Football Club, set out its ambition to build a new 32,000 seater stadium. The club's financial director stated that 'our ultimate strategy is to get into the top echelon of clubs in the Premier League and we see the new stadium as being central to that'. Explain how the development of a vision, mission and a set of long-term and short-term objectives would help Leicester City to achieve this 'ultimate strategy'. [20 marks]

Data response question – British Waterways

> British Waterways manages and cares for over 2000 miles of Britain's canals and rivers. British Waterways maintains canals for boating, angling and other uses. Work includes:
>
> - ensuring canals and rivers are safe places for people to enjoy;
> - maintaining locks, bridges, towing paths and the waterways themselves;
> - looking after the whole environment, i.e. buildings and wildlife that are associated with canals and rivers;
> - endeavouring to ensure there is the right amount of water in canals and rivers;
> - earning income from a wide range of waterway-related businesses to reinvest in the future of the waterways.
>
> The mission statement is:
>
> > 'Our business is to manage the inland waterway system efficiently for the increasing benefit of the United Kingdom. We aim to provide a safe and high quality environment for our customers, staff and local communities. We take a commercial approach and strive for excellence in every aspect of our work. The heritage and environment of our waterways will be conserved, improved and made to work well for future generations.'
>
> British Waterways also has a set of open objectives, including to:
>
> - continue the successful growth of waterways for leisure use;
> - improve the waterways' environmental and heritage value;
> - create an adequate and secure financial base;
> - promote profitable use of the waterways and maximise third-party investment from private, public and voluntary sectors;
> - eliminate the backlog of maintenance;
> - increase productivity.

1. How does a mission statement help an organisation like British Waterways to develop strategies? [8 marks]
2. What are open objectives? [2 marks]
3. How effective do you think British Waterways objectives are in helping the organisation to monitor ongoing performance? [5 marks]
4. How might British Waterways benefit from having more closed objectives? [5 marks]

Chapter Six

Choosing a strategy

*'The best strategy for any company is a strategy it can implement.
Before you choose one, think about what your company already does
well'.* Claudio Aspesi and Dev Vardhan

Strategic intent

The **strategic intent** of an organisation is the desired future state that it
is working towards. For example, in the case of Nestlé the strategic
intent is to become 'The World Food Company', and for Coca-Cola to
place its product 'within an arm's reach of desire' (the notion that
consumers will have worldwide access to Coca-Cola).

Every organisation needs to be clear about its strategic intent if it is to
plan ahead rather than simply to react to changes as and when they
occur. A truly successful strategy is one that matches what the
organisation is able to achieve within its environment. Nestlé and
Coca-Cola are able to meet the increasing demands from global
consumers because their profits and capital base enable ongoing
expansion.

Choosing a strategy

Strategic planning and **strategic management** both play a part in
choosing a strategy.

Strategic planning is the process of making strategic choices, while
managing is about producing the results from those choices.

Strategic planning enables managers to think their way to the
organisation they want.

The strategic plan deals with the most important question for the
organisation – 'where are we going and how are we going to get there?'

The end purpose of strategic planning is to gain a **competitive edge**
over rivals by **strategically positioning** your organisation in the right
markets at the right time, securing rapid and profitable growth during
good times, or survival in bad times.

An important part of developing a strategy is to develop clarity about
the relationship between the core and peripheral activities of the
organisation. The **core activities** are those which lie at the heart of the
organisation and its reason for being – e.g. to provide food products to
the world (in the case of Nestlé).

It is usually easy to identify the core activities of an organisation:

- because most of the profit and income of the organisation is tied up in these activities;
- because the image and identity of the organisation is associated with these activities; and
- because most of the time and resources (including people) are involved with these activities.

Peripheral activities are other activities that the organisation is involved in. It is essential that peripheral activities do not take up too much time or drain the resources of the organisation. The business guru, Michael Porter suggested in the 1970s that organisations should 'stick to the knitting' i.e. their core activities. A large number of successful businesses have followed this strategy.

The key features of **successful strategies** are that:

- They are based on what is happening in the organisation's environment. This means that planners have to understand their markets, opportunities, changes, trends and external threats.
- Strategies are concerned with the product or service mix to be produced or offered and the markets in which the products or services will be sold (this is referred to as the scope of the organisation).
- Strategies usually involve complex decisions that deal with considerable uncertainty.
- Strategies need to be flexible, to be able to alter with changing circumstances.
- Strategy is an ongoing process – strategies need to be updated and revised.
- Strategies seek to create improvements over time.
- Strategies are action plans for an organisation which help it to maximize its strengths within its environment.

Analysis, choice and implementation

Strategic planning and management consists of three major interlinking threads – strategic analysis, strategic choice and strategic implementation (Fig. 17).

While strategic analysis and choice are primarily concerned with strategic planning, the implementation of strategy is the concern of strategic management (and is the subject of Chapter 7).

In the previous chapter we saw that **strategic analysis** involved developing an understanding of the position of the organisation in

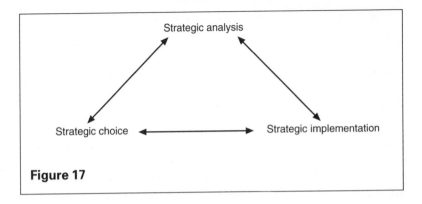

Figure 17

terms of its external environment, internal resources and competences, and the expectations and influences of stakeholders.

Once strategic planners have this understanding of factors guiding future strategy they are in a position to create a menu of options, which they can then evaluate and select from.

Preparing to make a choice

Factors to be taken into consideration when preparing to make a **strategic choice** include:

- Stakeholder expectations and influence – what do stakeholders want, and how much influence do they have over decision making?
- Mission and objectives of the organisation (this may need to be changed as a result of a change of strategic direction).
- The bases of competitive advantage of the organisation – choice of strategy needs to be based on the strengths of the organisation (relative to competitors).
- The resources and capabilities available to carry out the strategy (what the organisation is capable of).

Creating a menu of strategic options

It is important to create a **menu of strategic options** rather than to limit choice. The most obvious choice is not necessarily the best.

There are four broad types of strategy that organisations can choose:

1. Growth strategies

Growth is a common form of business strategy. It is likely to be pursued when an organisation has identified market opportunities and has the resources and capability available to exploit these opportunities. Growth is most likely to occur when the external environment is favourable, for example as a result in a growth in economic activity (boom period). Growth will occur when companies want to expand into new markets. For example, in the 21st century we have seen the growth of new markets in Eastern Europe, China, India and the Pacific Rim. Many European companies, e.g. oil companies, pharmaceutical companies, food manufacturers, etc., have expanded into these markets, as illustrated by Amstrad's move into the Chinese mobile phone market (see boxed article below).

Acquisitions, mergers, takeovers and **joint ventures** are all part of the growth process and involve taking over and developing joint arrangements with existing companies. In preparing a growth strategy, organisations will establish a set of objectives – related to areas such as market share, new product development, profits, turnover, etc.

Amstrad enters China's mobile phone market

Amstrad, the electronics group chaired by Sir Alan Sugar, yesterday announced it was moving into the mainland Chinese mobile phone market with a deal to have its phones manufactured locally.

Amstrad's shares rose 9p to 125p on the news it had delivered on its promise to take on mobile giants such as Motorola and Nokia, which control 90 per cent of the Chinese market.

The company's new low-cost phones will be manufactured under licence by Haier CCT, a company formed by Hong Kong's CCT Telecom and the leading mainland domestic appliance group, Haier.

Amstrad will receive an upfront design fee for the phones, and a licence payment enabling Haier CCT to sell the phones in China and Taiwan. Amstrad will also receive a royalties payment for each unit sold.

Martin Bland, finance director at Amstrad, said: 'We will get a slice of the growth side, which we believe to be substantial – 42 million mobile phones were sold in China last year. But we will not bear any of the risk.'

Mr Bland said he was confident that Haier CCT would be successful in taking market share away from existing Western providers in China, as it had already done this in the domestic appliances market.

Amstrad itself will sell the phones manufactured by Haier CCT in markets outside China and Taiwan, including Europe. Amstrad last year said it would be able to make significant cost savings by manufacturing phones in China.

The Independent, 13 February 2001, by Katherine Griffiths

2. Multinationalism

Sometimes **multinationalism** is seen as a separate strategy, and involves the process of moving beyond the domestic market to grow into overseas markets.

3. Retrenchment

Retrenchment involves cutting back activities away from niche or peripheral markets. The purpose here is to better enable an organisation to concentrate on its core activities to better focus its energies.

4. Diversification

Diversification is a strategy of moving into new activities in which the organisation has limited or no experience. There is usually a clear logic to diversification. For example, when Rupert Murdoch's media group moved into satellite and then digital television, they were doing so because they saw this as the next stage in media development. If they had remained in existing forms of terrestrial television and newsprint they might have gone the way of the dinosaurs. Diversification requires an organisation to develop new sets of competences and capabilities.

A distinction is often made between choosing a strategy which is based on 'fit' and one which is based on '**stretch**'. A business that builds strategies around 'fit' tries to adapts its resources to meet the needs of the market. In contrast, one that goes for 'stretch' recognises that it will need to adapt its resources and capabilities to meet the needs of the market – which often occurs in the case of differentiation.

Competitive strategies

Michael Porter argues that there are two main ways to gain competitive advantage. One of these is through differentiation and the other is through price. He argues that a company can seek to dominate a market by charging **low prices** and not offering much in the way of **differentiation**, for example, a cut-price supermarket, a cheap tub of margarine, a supermarket's own brand of beans, etc. The low-price producer will aim to sell in very large quantities using all the economies of low-cost production that are available (**low price strategy**). Alternatively, a firm can charge a higher price and produce a more differentiated product (**differentiation strategy**). The higher price enables the firm to cover the higher costs of production involved with differentiation (see boxed item on Tesco's strategy and Fig. 18 overleaf).

Tesco changes its competitive strategy

When Tesco first entered retailing they went for the low-price strategy. The motto of Tesco's founder, Jack Cohen was 'pile them high and sell them cheap'. He bought in bulk and sold at a low price. As time moved on, Tesco moved more and more up-market, moving away from low price to differentiation strategies. Tesco did this because they realised UK consumers were becoming better off and many of them were changing in their tastes away from cheap groceries. Tesco has thus effectively changed its strategy and resource base to better fit the changing retail environment.

Figure 18 Tesco moves upmarket

Porter shows that the best ways to make profits are not to be average. The low-cost firm can make higher than average profits by selling a lot more than rivals and employing economies of scale. The high-price firm too can make higher than average profits by selling a differentiated product that customers are willing to pay the premium price for. However, the average firm has nothing to differentiate themselves from rivals – and will make lower than average profits. Porter described the average firm as being '**stuck in the middle**'.

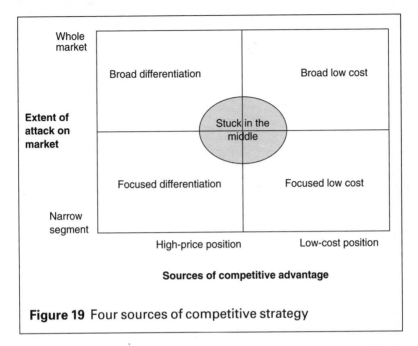

Figure 19 Four sources of competitive strategy

Porter identified four possible favourable competitive strategies (Fig. 19):

- **Broad differentiation strategy**: involves selling a differentiated product to the mass market. Coca-Cola does this – its product is differentiated through advertising and marketing as well as the product itself.
- **Focused differentiation strategy**: involves selling a differentiated product to a narrow market segment or niche market, rather than to a total market, e.g. a speciality high quality magazine.
- **Broad low cost strategy**: involves selling a largely undifferentiated product to a mass market using low cost to drive sales, e.g. bags of sugar with no frills packaging.
- **Focused low cost strategy**: involves selling an undifferentiated product or service to a smaller market segment, e.g. selling unbranded biscuits and sweets in a local market.

Ansoff's growth strategies

Igor **Ansoff's matrix** of strategic options, has been helpful in enabling strategists to consider options for growth. The matrix compares the alternative of developing new products and new markets (Fig. 20).

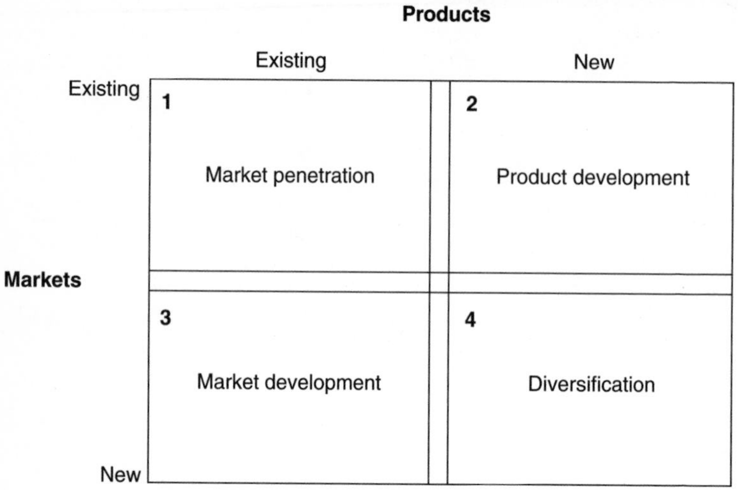

Figure 20 Ansoff's matrix of options for growth

In Fig. 20 the options are numbered from one to four in order of increasing risk:

1. Market penetration
This involves selling more of the same product to the same types of people. This is possible either by increasing market share at the expense of others, by developing a competitive advantage, or by growing the total market size. Currently, the market for mobile phones is one where companies are achieving growth as a result of total market growth.

2. Product development
This involves a company exploiting the strength of its relationship with customers and using its creative ability to develop new products suited to their needs. Supermarkets are a good example of this. They have gradually moved away from simply selling groceries to a wide range of other products including household goods, clothes, petrol, computers and even cars!

3. Market development

New customers can be more difficult to develop than products, but where an organisation has significant product strengths this can be a good opportunity for growth. Examples can include selling to export markets, or a different customer type. Lucozade, a high-energy drink was originally sold to speed recovery from illness, but the company developed a new market among sports people.

4. Diversification

This involves developing new expertise both in terms of product and markets and is the highest risk alternative. Often companies, rather than develop their own expertise, will buy another company to achieve their objectives. A recent example is the acquisition by the Ford Motor Company of the Kwik-Fit replacement car tyre and exhaust fitting company.

Choosing from the menu

The various strategic options which are available to an organisation need to be weighed up against each other. There are three important criteria for evaluating options:

- suitability
- acceptability
- feasibility.

Suitability concerns whether the strategies fit the situation. For example, tools such as PESTLE, SWOT, and competitor analyses provide a good view of the relationship between the internal organisation and the external environment. The organisation then needs to look at whether their strategic options provide a suitable use of resources in a given environment, for example, whether a strategy:

- fits with internal weaknesses or external threats facing an organisation
- builds on an organisation's existing strengths and environmental opportunities
- matches the organisation's stated objectives.

Acceptability is concerned with whether a strategy will be acceptable to the organisation and those with a significant interest in it. For example, is the level of risk acceptable and are shareholders and other stakeholders prepared to agree to the plans? They may have reservations based on what they consider to be ethical, fair and reasonable. For example, strategies involving high financial returns in a developing market may have to be shelved if influential stakeholders see the environmental costs as being too high a price to pay.

Feasibility is concerned with whether strategic plans can work in practice and primarily whether the organisation has adequate resources to carry out particular plans, for example whether:

- the funds are available
- the organisation will be able to sustain the required level of output
- the organisation will be able to deal with the competition that it generates
- it will be able to meet the required market share.

Choosing a corporate strategy therefore involves a range of considerations, in order to make sure that the option selected will work in practice.

KEY WORDS

Strategic intent	Fit
Strategic planning	Stretch
Strategic management	Competitive strategies
Competitive edge	Low price strategy
Strategic positioning	Differentiation strategy
Core activities	Stuck in the middle
Successful strategies	Broad differentiation strategy
Strategic analysis	Focused differentiation strategy
Strategic choice	Broad low cost strategy
Menu of strategic options	Focused low cost strategy
Growth strategies	Ansoff's matrix
Acquisitions	Market penetration
Mergers	Product development
Takeovers	Market development
Joint ventures	Suitability
Multinationalism	Acceptability
Retrenchment	Feasibility
Diversification	

Further reading

Johnson, G. and Scholes, K., Chapter 1, *Exploring Corporate Strategy*, sixth edition, Financial Times/Prentice Hall, 2001.

Pettinger, R., Chapter 5, *Introduction to Management*, Macmillan Business, third edition, 2001.

Thompson, J.L., Chapter 14, *Strategic Management*, Thomson Business Press, fourth edition, 2000.

Further references

Ansoff, H.I., *Corporate Strategy*, McGraw-Hill, 1965 (revised edition 1987).

Porter, M.E., *Competitive Advantage: Creating and sustaining superior performance*, Free Press, 1984.

Useful websites

Amstrad website: www.amstrad.com

Tesco website: www.tesco.com

Essay topics

1. (a) Using recent examples show how well-known organisations have used
       (i) growth, and
       (ii) retrenchment strategies.   [10 marks]
   (b) Explain why one of these organisations is likely to have chosen the strategy that it did.   [10 marks]
2. (a) How does Porter's identification, differentiation, and low costs strategies help to explain why some retailers are more successful than others?   [10 marks]
   (b) Explain why the choice of the strategy that Ansoff describes as 'diversification' would prove to be the most risky one for an existing company.   [10 marks]

Data response – The way forward for Cadbury-Schweppes

In February 2001, Cadbury-Schweppes, the maker of Dairy Milk chocolate and Dr Pepper soft drinks, was considering setting up a chain of branded cafés to help boost its presence in the static UK confectionery market. The Chief Executive, John Sunderland, told shareholders that he was determined to get the UK businesses momentum going again and that the company was looking at ways of increasing the availability of products to consumers. One idea was to roll-out its pilot Café Cadbury which had been successfully tried in Bath across many other locations, and installing vending machines in hospitals and pubs.

In 2000, Cadbury-Schweppes spent £1.5bn on acquisitions, and is continuing to look for expansion opportunities, for example the possible purchase of the French company Pernod Ricard's Orangina soft drinks unit.

The most obvious target for acquisition in February 2001 was the sweets division owned by Pfizer, the pharmaceutical company. It was known that Pfizer was looking to sell this business which mostly owns chewing-gum brands in the United States and Latin America.

1. What is an acquisition? [2 marks]
2. Why did Cadbury-Schweppes spend £1.5bn on acquisitions in 2000? [4 marks]
3. Why might setting up a chain of branded cafés prove a challenge to Cadbury-Schweppes when compared with alternative strategies that it might choose to pursue? [8 marks]
4. Why do you think that Cadbury-Schweppes has engaged in an expansion strategy? [6 marks]

Chapter Seven

Implementing and monitoring strategies

'A prescriptive corporate strategy is one where the objective has been defined in advance and the main elements have been developed before the strategy commences ... Emergent corporate strategy is a strategy whose final objective is unclear and whose elements are developed during the course of its life, as the strategy proceeds.'
Richard Lynch

It would be nice to think that managers could prescribe a strategy for an organisation and then implement the strategy to meet organisational objectives in a planned way.

A prescriptive view of corporate strategy

A **prescriptive view** of corporate strategy is based on considerable confidence in the ability of managers to manage the organisation into a desired future state. The starting point is to agree on an objective for the organization, e.g. a given return on capital employed. The organisational environment is then analysed in order to generate a series of forecasts identifying the organisation's potential for success in the future given the forecasted environment. A series of strategic options can then be placed on a menu for decision makers who then choose the 'best' option. This option is then implemented.

Strategic implementation involves developing the strategies, policies and operational planning procedures to translate strategy into action steps and then carrying out the required actions. Strategies then need to be monitored and evaluated to ensure ongoing improvement. The list of steps outlined below shows how strategies can be translated down into procedures. However, it is important to recognise that in a modern dynamic business environment considerable flexibility needs to be built into strategic implementation to enable the organisation to respond to change.

Corporate strategies are made at the level of the whole organisation/company. These strategies are then translated into a series of **generic** and **competitive strategies** for each business unit, and good/market.

Functional strategies (if the organisation is organised on a functional basis) are designed to carry out the competitive strategies and these will be translated into a series of action plans. Functional strategies will be designed to build on the distinctive competences of the organisation that give competitive advantage. For example, a large pharmaceutical company might have developed corporate and business unit strategies designed to achieve market leadership; translated down into a functional strategy for the research and development function this might involve a strategy of technological leadership through the pioneering of new innovations such as research and development of new treatments for cancer.

Policies are broad guidelines for decision making that link the formulation of strategy with its implementation. Organisations use policies to make sure that employees throughout the organisation make decisions and take actions that support the corporate mission, objectives and strategies. For example, the pharmaceutical company involved in cancer research may have a policy of not testing its research on animals. Sometimes referred to as **operational planning**, strategy implementation involves day-to-day decisions in resource allocation.

A **programme** is a statement of the activities or steps needed to accomplish a single-use plan. It makes the strategy action-oriented. Our pharmaceutical company may establish a specific programme of research activities for its cancer treating drugs.

A **budget** is a statement of an organisation's programmes in terms of finance. Used in planning and control, a budget lists the detailed costs of each programme, e.g. a specific budget for cancer research testing.

Procedures, sometimes termed **Standard Operating Procedures** (SOPs) are a system of sequential steps or techniques that describe in detail how a particular task or job is to be done. They typically detail the various activities that must be carried out in order to complete the corporation's programmes. Operational planners at our pharmaceutical company will draw up a sequential list of SOPs for its cancer research programme.

The relationship between strategy and structure

The structure and design of the organisation is essential to the implementation of successful strategy. The organisational structure needs to be clear and everyone needs to know where strategic and operational decisions are made.

The **structure** of an organisation is the pattern of relationships among positions in an organisation and among members of the organisation. The purpose of structure is the division of work among members of the organisation, and the co-ordination of their activities so they are directed towards achieving the aims and objectives of the organisation.

Much has been written about the relationship between the strategy and the structure of an organisation. Clearly there needs to be a close fit between strategy and structure for successful strategic implementation to take place. Lawrence and Lorsch (1967) argued that the organisation should be structured in such a way that it can respond to pressures for change from its environment and pursue any appropriate opportunities which are spotted.

In a classic study of large US corporations such as DuPont, General Motors, and Standard Oil, Alfred Chandler concluded that structure follows strategy – that is, changes in corporate strategy lead to changes in organisational structure.

The structure must therefore be capable of implementing strategies, and in this way can be seen as the means by which an organisation seeks to achieve its strategic objectives. The structure must be capable of formulating and implementing strategy.

The structure of the organisation can thus be designed to break down the operations that are required to implement strategies. The organisation will be structured into a series of divisions, business units or functions. The people that make up these sub-structures will be working to objectives, targets, plans, programmes, policies and procedures which give them a direction for their activities (Fig. 21).

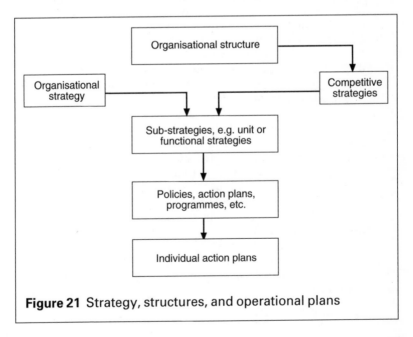

Figure 21 Strategy, structures, and operational plans

Altering structures at Marks & Spencer in line with the new strategy

Marks & Spencer won the award for retailer of the year in 1994, but by the end of the decade it was clear that the company was losing touch with many of its customers leading to a fall in profits of 23 per cent in 1998. In 1999, therefore M&S developed a new 'leading standards' strategy to win back customers. The Annual Report for 2000 declared that 'every process is now guided by the customer imperative'. M&S decided that by listening to their customers and giving them what they want, they can turn around their business and regain some of their former success.

The strategy involved a number of changes to the stores and to the range of products offered. It also involved a change in the structure of the business to deliver this greater customer focus. Key changes in structure were:

- **Customer business units**. Restructuring of the way in which units work has provided M&S with Customer Business Units. These units, which are basically involved with buying, selling and marketing, provide the company with an integrated approach to these areas. They share resources and provide M&S with a flatter structure with which to make faster decisions to help give the customers what they want and how they want it.
- **Customer insight unit**. A specific unit set up to find out who the customers are and what they want. In recent times, M&S have undertaken extensive research and have responded to their findings to provide customers with more of what they want. They have carried out the largest survey of women's sizes in the UK and have changed their sizing accordingly. A series of TV adverts, 'I'm normal', were the result of this. Other actions that were taken in response to customer needs were the moving of the children's wear department to the ground floor to provide easy access for parents with pushchairs, and reduced APR on credit cards.
- **Reducing layers of hierarchy**. The ratios of managers to staff in the stores have been halved from 6:1 to 12:1. This lessens administration time and gives the shop floor staff more responsibility for decision making. Also the structure of the shop floor staff has changed in that there are no surpervisors and deputy supervisors, everyone is equal in a team of sales advisors. Although there are still leaders within these teams they do not have that title.

Of course, the translation of corporate strategy into individual actions is not and should not be seen as a simple, static, and one-way process. Rather, it is a complex, dynamic and multi-directional process. As we have seen earlier, strategy formulation is an adaptive process responding to changes within and outside the organisation. Changes at lower levels within the organisation will lead to new developments in functional, competitive and in turn corporate strategies.

We use the term **strategic architecture** to refer to the process of building sets of interlinking competences that will enable the organisation to develop competitive advantage. Organisations need to identify the main sources of competitive advantage in the sector or market segment that they are operating in, e.g. having the fastest distribution links, the most rapid response to consumer requirements, the most reliable components, etc. They then need to design and build the core competences which enable them to win and maintain competitive advantage – the strategic architecture.

For example, the supermarket chain Safeway have recently (2001) developed a 'reinventing strategy' to focus on the competencies which they see as being particularly successful in driving competitive advantage. There are four elements to this strategy:

- 'Product and price', concentrates on making deep price cuts on selected products – giving competitive advantage in terms of value for money.
- 'Be best at fresh', involves seeking competitive advantage through offering fresher and more appealing bread, vegetables, fruit, etc., than rivals.
- 'Be best at availability' involves ensuring 100 per cent availability of their top-selling products. Investment in the latest supply chain technology enables Safeway to see exactly what products are moving off the shelves and to replace them as and when required.
- 'Be best at customer service' involves making sure that staff have the right training to ensure that customers feel that they are getting the best possible service.

The relationship between strategy and resources

There are two possible approaches to resource planning: 'fit' and 'stretch'.

A business that builds strategies around 'fit' tries to adapt its resources to meet the needs of the market. One that goes for 'stretch' is more likely to break the mould because it looks for new opportunities to exploit its core competences and also adapts resources to create market need.

Breaking the mould may happen in a culture in which people feel free to experiment or where competences that lead to competitive advantage have been identified.

Whatever the type of strategy selected, the organisation must plan to use resources efficiently and to work with or adjust the culture.

Closing the strategic gap

The **strategic gap** is the difference which exists at any one time between the capabilities of the organisation and the most significant environmental factors (Fig. 22). The strategic gap reflects the imbalance between the current strategic position of the organisation and its desired strategic position. The gap is measured by comparing the organisation's capabilities with the opportunities and threats in its external environment.

A **capability profile** establishes the principal capabilities of the organisation. The four main areas of weakness and strength include:

- Management – the extent to which existing management has a good decision-making track record.
- Technology – the extent to which the organisation keeps up with state-of-the-art developments in its field.
- Policies – the extent to which there are clear and well-focused policies covering all aspects of the organisation's activities.
- Resources – the extent to which the organisation has the right balance of the relevant resources.

The **environmental assessment** examines:

- Opportunities – situations with a potential to enhance the competitive position of the organisation. Clearly, opportunities need to be matched with capabilities.

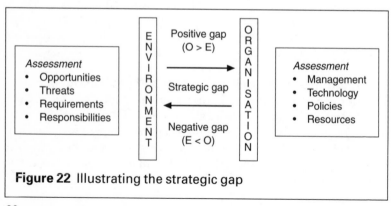

Figure 22 Illustrating the strategic gap

- Threats – there are a range of threats but the most common are competition and technological obsolescence.
- Requirements – include statutory requirements, legal codes and other government-related restrictions on strategic choices.
- Responsibilities – consist of expectations on the part of stakeholder groupings including social responsibilities.

A positive strategic gap exists when O>E. In this situation the organisation is well placed to exploit opportunities, cope with threats, or meet requirements and responsibilities in the external environment.

A negative strategic gap exists when E<O. This requires management actions to reverse the gap because the organisation is unable to take up opportunities, respond to threats, or its responsibilities and requirements in the external environment.

Perhaps, the best state of affairs for an organisation is one in which O = E because the organisation is in tune with its environment and is taking up appropriate opportunities, responding to threats as and when they arise, and dealing effectively with its requirements and responsibilities.

Intended, realised, and emergent strategies

It would be convenient if an organisation had complete mastery of the development of its strategies. The reality is far removed from this (Fig. 23).

The strategic planning process enables an organisation to choose a strategy which can be regarded as its **intended strategy**. However, in the

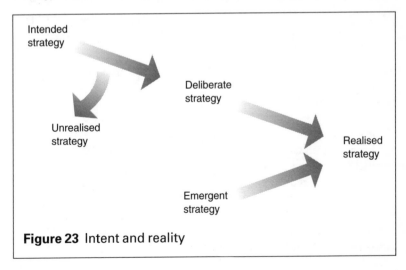

Figure 23 Intent and reality

course of time, unforeseen events take place which force the organisation to abandon some of its original intentions (**unrealised strategies**) and to take on board new elements of strategy (emergent strategies) which are not what the organisation originally intended. The strategy which materialises in the real world is thus a combination of **realised strategies** and emergent strategies; i.e. a combination of elements of intended strategy which work in practice, and new elements of strategy which emerge along the way.

For example, in the late 1990s the UK chemical company ICI decided that it would sell off its old heavy polluting chemical plant (making bulk products such as fertiliser and gunpowder) and use the funds from its divestments to purchase new modern chemical plant (making sensory chemical products such as eye liners and lip glosses). Unfortunately, while ICI was able to purchase the new sensory chemical manufacturers (realised strategy), it had great difficulty in selling off its old plant because anti-monopoly legislation in the US prevented prospective buyers in the US from buying the ICI plant. ICI was therefore forced to borrow large sums of money (**emergent strategy**) to bridge the gap.

Emergent strategy

There are a number of views on the extent to which strategy can be tightly planned. A number of writers on strategy such as Ansoff are seen to belong to a 'design school of strategic management' suggesting that strategy can be deliberately managed in a logical sequence of steps.

In contrast Mintzberg and others see strategy as 'emerging' over time involving an element of trial and error. Strategy emerges, adapting to human needs and continuing to develop over time. Managers are not fully able to prescribe strategy because:

- They are only capable of handling a selected number of strategic options at a time.
- They perceive data in a biased way.
- They are more likely to seek satisfactory solutions rather than maximise the objectives of the organisation.
- Organisations consist of coalitions of people formed into power blocks. Strategy formulation is likely to come from compromise between different power blocks rather than being made by a single managerial group seeking to achieve a common set of objectives.
- Decision making relies on the culture, routines, and politics of an organisation as much as on rational decision making.

And, of course because decision makers are human they are likely to make mistakes. Gary Hamel and C.K. Prahalad, in *Competing for the Future*, show that 'every manager carries around in his or her head a set of biases, assumptions, and presuppositions about the structure of the relevant 'industry', about how one makes money in the industry, about who the competition is and isn't, about who the customers are and aren't, about which technologies are viable and which aren't and so on'.

For the strategist, this **'theory of the business'** acts both as a guide and as a constraint on thought processes. The best-laid strategies may fail when management's map fails to chart the realities of the business situation – when one or more of management's assumptions, premises or beliefs are incorrect, or when loose thinking renders the overall 'theory of the business' no longer valid.

The importance of leadership in implementing strategy

In terms of the creation of strategies, the stakeholders of organisations seek some sort of **directive leadership** from senior managers. The responsibility of the **senior management team** within an organisation is to create strategy (after a wide process of consultation) and then to set out the structures for implementing the strategy.

Research indicates that the happiest, most productive employees are those who feel empowered at work. Good leaders need to coach and motivate and then leave people to get on with it in terms of the grass roots implementation of strategies.

Strategic decisions are those concerned with creating the overall direction for an organisation while operational ones are concerned with the day-to-day implementation of routine decisions within the organisation. Some organisations use a system called **'red, amber and green'** for team decision making. If a policy is red, it's not up for debate; amber means 'please discuss this before implementing it'; green means 'you're in charge, follow your judgement'. In a good team, about ten per cent of decisions will be red, 20 per cent amber and 70 per cent green.

Johnson and Scholes identify a number of **management styles** which are appropriate in managing strategic change in different circumstances (Table 3).

The importance of communication in implementing strategy

Effective **communication systems** are needed to make sure that everyone within the organisation shares the vision, mission, objectives

Table 3 Management styles identified by Johnson and Scholes

Style	Approach	Circumstances
Education and communication	Group briefings	Incremental change (or long-term radical change)
Participation/ collaboration	Involvement in creating strategies	
Intervention	Change agent co-ordinates and delegates elements of change	Incremental or non-crisis transformational change
Direction	Use of authority to set direction and means of change	Transformational change
Coercion	Explicit use of power through command	Crisis/rapid transformational change in autocratic culture

and values and has a good grasp of the strategy and how it relates to their own efforts. Where an organisation is decentralised (as is the case in many organisations today) an effective communications network is required for feeding information around the organisation, and to ensure effective control. **Multi-channel flows** (in which information and ideas flow in all directions) of communication are helpful in creating a shared sense of ownership of corporate strategy.

Taking up a strategic position

To gain competitive advantage in the market place the organisation needs to do more than simply implement the same sort of strategy as its rivals. Michael Porter argues that competitive strategy is about being different. It means deliberately choosing a different set of activities to deliver a unique mix of value. He believes that organisations need to do more that be operationally efficient. Your rivals can become operationally efficient by copying your ideas. Strategy is all about making yourself different. Porter argues that the essence of strategy is

setting limits. A company must set limits on what it is trying to achieve in the marketplace; what value it is trying to deliver to whom.

Strategic positions according to Porter come from three sources (each involving a different set of limits). One is to limit the product or service that a company offers (variety based positioning). A second is to limit the customers served based on their need (needs based positioning). The third, is to limit the customers served based on their accessibility (access based positioning).

- **Variety based positioning**. This involves producing a distinct subset of an industry's product or services. For example, QuickFit in this country concentrates on supplying customers with replacement exhaust pipes, replacement tyres, and breaks etc, rather than providing a full range of repairs for motor vehicles. QuickFit concentrates on being the best at the distinct set of activities involved in this line of work.
- **Needs based positioning**. This involves meeting most or all of the needs of a particular group of customers. IKEA, for example, set out to provide for all the home and furnishing needs of people looking for relatively cheap and functional home products.
- **Access based positioning**. This involves focusing on customers that are accessible in a chosen way. For example, in the US Carmike Cinemas operates cinemas in cities and towns with populations under 200,000. Operating efficiently in these locations requires a different configuration of activities than in large urban areas, and Carmike has developed expertise in these activities through specialisation.

Contingency planning

This chapter has shown that it is difficult to be prescriptive about strategy. Uncertainty is everywhere and organisations need to be ready to cope with change. **Contingency planning** involves making 'what if' plans just in case something goes wrong. If strategies don't work out as expected it is important to have fallback plans to help the organisation to steer its way to the future. Contingency planning involves continually questioning current methods and assumptions and preparing alternative actions should forecasts be different to what is expected.

Control, monitoring and evaluating chosen strategies

The assessment of actual performance in the light of strategic plans is an essential part of the strategic planning cycle and should provide feedback to teach of the key stages in strategy creation.

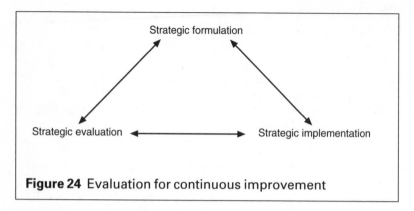

Figure 24 Evaluation for continuous improvement

Evaluation is not only a control device, but is also a means of making continuous improvement to strategy formulation and implementation (Fig. 24).

When organisations are creating new strategies therefore they also need to be creating the processes which will enable them to evaluate these strategies. The notion of benchmarking is helpful in strategic evaluation. A **benchmark** is a selected measure for comparison. For example, a benchmark for quality might be the standards set by the leading company in a particular industry. A benchmark for production might be the record figure achieved by a company with its existing production plant, etc. The implication of benchmarking is that organisations are actively seeking to identify the best possible standards within the organisation and within the organisational environment in order to lead the field.

A control tool is a mechanism for controlling a plan or activity. If performance does not meet the required standard then actions are put in place to rectify the situation.

Control needs to take place at three levels within the organisation:

- strategic level control
- management level control
- operational level control.

Control is an important part of the strategy process. Control processes make it possible to check that objectives have been met, and to make adjustments to strategy as and when appropriate. Peter Drucker believes that to be able to control performance a manager needs to be clear about objectives and must be able to measure performance and results against these objectives. Therefore managers need clear and common measurements in all areas of business. These measurements need not be rigidly quantitative, nor need they be exact. But they have to be clear, simple and rational. They have to be relevant and direct attention and efforts where they should go. They have to be reliable and understandable.

The sorts of analysis that an organisation will need for control purposes would include the items in Table 4.

Each manager should have the information he or she needs to measure performance and should receive it soon enough to make any changes necessary for the desired results. This information should go to the manager directly and not to their superior. It should be the means of self-control, not a tool of control from above.

The creation of objectives, and systematic appraisal of performance, and measurement of performance enables the general aims of the organisation to be translated down into operational programmes and activities which can be controlled by individuals at all levels within the organisation.

This chapter has shown that there are a number of stages involved in implementing and evaluating strategies. In predictable situations it is possible to prescribe strategies which can then be broken down into subsets of approaches for implementing the strategy right down to

Table 4 Analysis necessary for an organization to take control

Analysis of	Used to control
Financial analysis	
Ratio analysis	Aspects of solvency, liquidity, profitability
Variance analysis	Costs and revenues
Cash budgeting	Cash flows
Capital budgeting	Investment
Market analysis	
Market share analysis	Competitive position
Market research information	Types of goods and services offered
Sales analysis	
Sales budgets	Effectiveness of selling
Human resource analysis	
Labour turnover	Workforce stability
Work/output measurement	Productivity
Physical resource analysis	
Product inspection	Quality

operational action plans. In the real world of course, strategic plans run into unexpected difficulties often caused by changes in the environment. Control tools and contingency plans therefore need to be devised to maximise the effectiveness of strategies and to develop new strategies to cope with changing situations.

KEY WORDS

Prescriptive view	Emergent strategy
Strategic implementation	Unrealised strategy
Generic strategies	Theory of the business
Competitive strategies	Directive leadership
Functional strategies	Senior management team
Policies	Red, amber and green
Operational planning	Management styles
Programme	Communication systems
Budget	Multi-channel flows
Standard operating procedures	Setting limits
Structure	Strategic positions
Strategic architecture	Variety based positioning
Fit	Needs based positioning
Stretch	Access based positioning
Strategic gap	Contingency planning
Capability profile	Evaluation
Environmental assessment	Benchmark
Intended strategy	Control
Realised strategy	

Further reading

Johnson, G. and Scholes, K., Chapters 2 and 9, *Exploring Corporate Strategy*, sixth edition, Financial Times/Prentice Hall, 2000.

Lynch, R., Chapter 17, *Corporate Strategy*, Pitman Publishing, second edition, 2000.

Needham, D. & Dransfield, R., Chapters 29 and 30, *Business for Higher Awards*, second edition, 2000.

Thompson, J.L., *Strategic Management*, Chapter 19, Thomson Business Press, 2000.

Additional References

Ansoff, H.I., *Corporate Strategy*, Penguin, 1987.

Chandler, A.D., *Strategy and Structure: Chapters in the history of the American Industrial Enterprise*, MIT Press, 1962.

Drucker, P.F., The coming of the new organisation, *Harvard Business Review*, January-February, 1988.

Hamel, G., and Prahalad, C.K., Strategy as stretch and leverage, *Harvard Business Review*, March-April, 1993.

Hamel, G. ,and Prahalad, C.K., Competing for the future, *Economist Conference*, June, 1994.

Lawrence, P.R. and Lorsch, J.W., *Organisation and Environment*, Richard D. Irwin, 1967.

Mintzberg, H., *The Structuring of Organisations*, Prentice-Hall, 1979.

Porter, M.E., What is Strategy, Chapter 4, in ed. Segal-Horne, S., *The Strategy Reader*, Blackwell Business, second edition, 2000.

Useful website

Marks & Spencer: www.marksandspencer.com
Safeway: www.safeway.com

Essay questions

1. Is the strategy that an organisation chooses always the same one that it is able to implement? Discuss with examples.   [20 marks]
2. (a) How can an organisation seek to improve on the strategy that it is currently implementing?   [10 marks]
   (b) Explain the role of the following in the implementation of strategy:
      (i)   the structure of the organization   [4 marks]
      (ii) organisational resources   [3 marks]
      (iii) leadership   [3 marks]

Data response

In 2000 Marks and Spencer made a radical shift in its strategy to place far more emphasis on the customer. A number of aspects of the implementation of the new strategy have a direct effect on employees:

- Maximised use of skills on the basis of 'best fit'. Job roles have been redefined so that that there is scarcely anyone with the same job description as they had one year earlier. Employees have been moving to where their 'best fit' is, based on assessment of their skills and how best these skills can be used to serve the customer.
- Decision making by the best informed. Where previously decision making had been done by the most senior staff, now the decisions are made by the 'best informed', i.e. those who have the best knowledge about the issues and who may not necessarily be the most senior.

- Empowerment of sales floor staff. Due to the extra numbers of employees on the shop floor and fewer managers in charge, all the customer facing staff have more responsibility for 'on the spot' decision making. They have power to make decisions on all customer care issues, for example whether to make refunds or exchange goods.
- Customer-focused teams. The team structure has changed to coincide with the delayering and the extra customer facing employees. Where supervisors used to cooperate, team leaders now share responsibilities across departments.
- 'Realising the benefit' training for all staff. Each staff member is given four hours of training to decide which is their best fit role, what their special skills are and how to get on with implementing the new strategy.

1. What is the relationship between the changes described above and the new M&S corporate strategy? [5 marks]
2. How would M&S be able to evaluate the success of:
   (a) the new strategy [3 marks]
   (b) the changes described in the case study. [4 marks]
3. Why did M&S need to change its structure in order to implement the new strategy? [5 marks]
4. What style of management do you think would be most appropriate to introduce the changes outlined in the case study? [3 marks]

Chapter Eight

Managing change in the organisation

'One should think of change as a stage to be managed, with targets and assigned change managers.' Edgar H. Schein

The origin and nature of change

Today the emphasis in most organisations is on successfully managing change. Managers need to be strategically aware of threats and opportunities which exist in the organisational environment and continually seek to improve the fit between the environment and the organisation's resources.

There are two major types of change which are particularly important in relation to corporate strategy.

Radical change is concerned with major alterations in an organisation and/or its component systems. For example, in recent years we have seen many organisations make major strategic shifts involving an investment in Internet technology – exemplified for example, by the way in which the retailer Iceland changed its name to Iceland.Com. High Street banks too have changed the way they operate to focus more on telephone, cash machine and computer banking services. Other examples of radical changes include the way in which many football clubs have moved from cramped inner city locations to areas where there is room for larger stadiums, easy access and room for better car parking facilities. For some organisations radical change may mean a radical retrenchment of business activity to focus on the core lines which yield the best prospects of good returns to the organisation as in the case of Future Network (see boxed text overleaf).

Incremental change is ongoing change that takes place as part of an organisation's ongoing evolution and development. Incremental change should be based on ongoing analysis and evaluation of strategies and of the changing environment to make steady improvements, e.g. in the way that Premier football clubs in recent years have improved their marketing, sponsorship and media links.

The success of change initiatives in organisations is dependent on the **change agents** (individuals and groups responsible for managing change) in the organisation. All modern managers need to have the skills to act as change agents to enable their organisation to move forward. Managers should be able to:

Future Network to close 20 titles with loss of 350 jobs worldwide

Future Network, the publisher of specialist consumer magazines, such as *Total Film* and *PC Gamer*, is to close 20 under-performing titles and cut its internet spending, with the loss of 350 jobs worldwide.

It has also appointed Morgan Stanley Dean Witter to 'explore options for the next stage of development of *Business 2.0*'. This US-based magazine is one of Future Network's most popular publications, with a circulation of 350,000, but it has suffered in recent months from a downturn in dot.com advertising, which has hit revenues. The business is thought to be worth about £150m. At yesterday's closing share price of 91p, down 14p, that is more than the market value of the whole of Future Network.

Future Network, whose non-executive directors include Elisabeth Murdoch, has issued three profit warnings in the past six months.

Chris Anderson, Future's founder and chairman, said: 'The company has spent the last 16 years building ... media brands. On a personal level, I'm deeply disappointed we are now having to cut back our efforts and let people go. But tougher times require tough measures, and this is absolutely the right decision for Future.'

In the UK, the six magazines earmarked for closure include *WAP*, *Digital Camera User* and *Quick and Easy Windows*. The reduction of Future's internet activity will result in the loss of 75 jobs in Britain and the US as five websites disappear.

The wind-down process is expected to be completed within three months. The closures will reduce investment spending by £5m, to below £15m. One-time restructuring costs are expected to be less than £5m.

The group is forecast to register an operating loss of £1m on turnover of £253m when it posts full-year results on 19 March. Internet spending in the period is expected to have reached £7m.

The Independent, 17 February 2001, by Lucy Baker

- identify the need for change
- be open to good ideas for change
- be able to successfully implement change.

The term **punctuated equilibrium** is used to describe situations in which over time strategy will alternate between periods of incremental and radical change (Fig. 25).

The necessity for change

Many business writers argue that the right time to change is 'all the time'. In other words, organisations should create a vision supported by a strategy which is then continuously monitored in order to regularly update the vision and strategy.

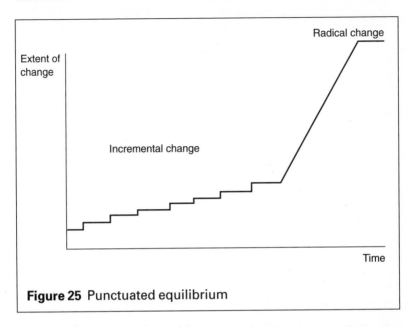

Figure 25 Punctuated equilibrium

Charles Handy in his book *The Empty Raincoat* (1995) identified the **Sigmoid Curve** as a useful illustration of when organisations should make changes. The Sigmoid Curve is simply the familiar S shape on its side (Fig. 26).

The upward path of the S curve indicates the time when the organisation appears to be most successful. Everyone is given a pat on the back. Sales and profits are increasing as is market share.

The organisation appears to be leading the field. However, Handy argues that it is at this point that things may already have started to go wrong. Handy argues that at point A on the curve (Fig. 26) the organisation may have peaked and be on the edge of a downswing.

Therefore at point B on the curve the organisation should make key strategic and structural changes. If the organisation does this in an intelligent way it can create an ongoing and sustained period of growth.

In many situations today the environment in which the organisation exists is turbulent and unpredictable. Organisations therefore need to have flexible planning structures, and the management vision for the future of the organisation may need to be adapted to changing situations.

Visionary leadership within the organisation is often helpful in aiding the organisation to successfully steer the path to change coupled with formal planning procedures.

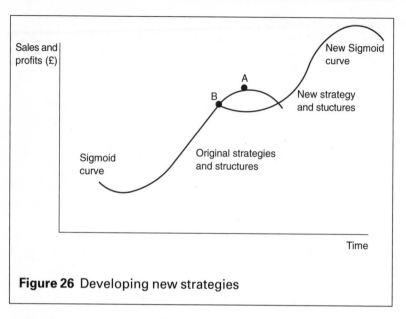

Figure 26 Developing new strategies

However, some writers believe that strong leadership from the centre and formal planning procedures are not sufficient to manage change strategies within an organisation.

For example, Ralph Stacey (1993) argues that in turbulent times organisations cannot just rely on formally planned strategies. He makes the case that '**adaptive strategies**' should be allowed to emerge from networks within the organisation responding to a changing environment.

Other writers such as James B. Quinn (1980) argue that strategic change should take place through a process of **logical incrementalism**. What is required is a broad strategy with a clearly defined mission for the organisation but to allow the detail of strategy to develop over time in line with changing circumstances. Quinn suggests that organisations are better off testing out relatively small changes and developing with this approach rather than to plan major changes in detail. For example, companies might test out new product lines in selected markets, before extending them on a larger scale. Teamworking and shared learning between managers is an important part of an incremental approach to strategic change.

Managing the change process

A number of steps need to be carried out in preparing for organisational change:

- Identify the change required. This can be done through a diagnostic approach. The change agents will need to communicate the nature of the change to all concerned, so at this stage it is important to be able to prepare a clear, concise statement of what is required.
- Set out the strengths and weaknesses of the organisation. A key question is whether the organisation is ready for change. Clearly there will be existing strengths (e.g. departments that will benefit from the change and who may have already had similar experience of making changes). It is important to show how the change fits with existing practices as well as identifying necessary improvement. Where weaknesses are identified, then resources and time may need to be put into these areas to make sure that the change works.
- Environmental analysis. Alterations to the organisational environment are likely to have played a major part in necessitating the change. These need to be identified so that people within the organisation do not perceive the changes as being purely a management whim. Changes in the environment provide opportunities to be grasped. Threats should be highlighted as real dangers to the organisation and its employees.
- Key individuals. It is essential to win support from those with most power in the organisation, in particular paying close attention to formal and informal power structure. The more people who can be made to take 'ownership' of structural changes the better. It is helpful to select individuals to 'champion' the change – the more influential these people are the better. The benefits of the change should be emphasised. The change agents should illustrate ways in which new structures and systems use existing knowledge and practice. The surprises should be minimised by consulting with and involving as many people as possible in the organisation.
- Identify the obstacles. In particular it is necessary to explore the concerns of individuals and groups. Time spent building up trust and support, and explaining the positive benefits is not wasted. Clear objectives and a timetable should be communicated to all those involved. People can be prepared for change by means of training courses and development programmes.
- Ways of recording the changes. Methods should be identified at the outset rather than waiting until the process of change has started.
- Evaluation. It is essential to evaluate the results in order to show how successful the change has been. At first, people may not be convinced that the change was worthwhile, so concrete evidence is helpful. The results should be communicated in newsletters, in meetings on the company website, etc.

Unfreezing, change and refreezing

Kurt Lewin recommends that a change process should involve key steps.

- **Unfreezing** – involves getting people and things ready to make the change.
- **Changing** – the process of implementing the change.
- **Refreezing** – making sure that the changes that have been carried out 'stick'.

Unfreezing

The unfreezing process involves preparing for change in the way described in the previous section. It is important for managers to continually monitor the fit between the organisation's capabilities, strategy and environment and be prepared to unfreeze the organisation to allow change to take place. Where changes in the environment are rapid the need for change is obvious. However, where change is less obvious it is easy to be caught out – leading to what is referred to as the boiled frog phenomenon. If a frog is placed into a pan of boiling water it will immediately jump out. However, place the frog in a pan of cold water and then very gradually raise the temperature and the frog will slowly boil to death. Organisations therefore need to constantly monitor changes in temperature (their environment) to make appropriate change responses.

Changing

Managing the process of change can be broken down into four elements (Fig. 27).

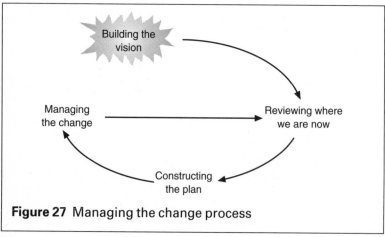

Figure 27 Managing the change process

Building the vision involves making people clear about what a particular change involves and how they are involved in it. Questions to be asked include:

- What is involved – that is, what is the proposed change?
- Why should we do it?
- What will the major effects be?
- How can we manage the change?

Reviewing where we are now involves assessments of the following:

- Current provisions.
- Resources.
- Roles and responsibilities.
- Development needs.
- The climate for change in the organisation.

Constructing the plan involves:

- The planning process.
- A policy statement.
- Action plans for implementing the change.
- Getting all parties committed to the change.

Once it is decided who is involved, what is involved and how the change is to be made, the next step is to put the plans into action and manage the change. It is necessary to:

- Manage the people involved.
- Check on and record progress.
- Overcome problems during implementation.
- Make sure that the change is permanent.
- Evaluate the change.
- Improve on any weak areas.

Refreezing
Refreezing is the process of maintaining the momentum of the change, by increasing the support for the change strategy and dealing with any difficulties that might arise. Evaluation is a key part of this process – using data to show the effectiveness of the new strategy.

Resistance to change
Resistance to change is an attitude or behaviour that reflects an unwillingness to make or support a proposed change.

There are a number of possible barriers. Some of these barriers are organisational barriers while others stem from resistance among individuals.

The main types of **organisational barriers** are:

- **Structural inertia.** Over time organisational structure has developed set patterns and procedures. These have become the norm and are embedded in the culture of the organisation. For example, in a hierarchical organisation, people will have become used to top-down decision making and communication patterns. It will not be easy to shift these structural patterns.
- **Existing power structures.** Power within an organisation will be embedded in an established way of doing things. To change an organisation and its existing strategies will inevitably involve a clash with the existing power structure. For example, in seeking to create a more democratic way of doing things in an organisation, there will inevitably be clashes with those who resist losing autocratic powers.
- **Resistance from work groups.** Over time work groups develop cultures and patterns of doing things. These work groups will be hostile to new patterns which threaten existing relationships and work practices.
- **The failure of previous change initiatives.** Within organisations there will be a collective memory of previous initiatives that failed and which led to bitterness, demotivation and waste of time. This memory of previous failures may lead groups within an organisation to develop a cynicism about the value of change.

The main types of **individual barriers** are:

- **Fears about the impact of the change on individuals and families.** Change strategies may lead to downsizing and redundancies and to the change in working patterns which may well impinge on the job security and social relationships for individuals and families.
- **Fears about having to increase commitment to the organisation.** New work practices and processes may require higher levels of commitment from individuals. They may not want to see their working lives take on greater significance.
- **Fear of the unknown.** Most people feel insecure when asked to face new situations which they are not familiar with.
- **Tradition and set ways.** Where people's jobs have changed little over time they may develop a conservative approach to work. They may therefore see change as threatening.
- **Loyalty to existing relationships.** People often develop a fondness for existing management structures and patterns of doing things.

They may resent being asked to change what they do or who they work with.

- **Failure to accept or recognise the need for change.** When people feel that what they are already doing is successful, they will be reluctant to work in a new way, if they see that 'there is no need for it'.

Strategies to overcome resistance to change

A number of approaches can be applied to deal with resistance to change.

- **Participation and involvement** is all about encouraging people to feel ownership for the change. The more people that are involved in making the change successful the better.
- **Education and communication** involves getting the message across through discussion, meetings, presentations, workshops, newsletters, etc. If people understand the need for the change and what is involved they are most likely to give their support.
- **Counselling and support** involves listening to people's views about the change, and the difficulties that it will present to them. Support involves finding ways to address the real needs of the individuals who feel threatened or unhappy about the change.
- **Negotiation** involves providing agreed incentives to encourage people to accept the change, e.g. pay bonuses for improved performance.
- **Manipulation** involves seeking to influence people, for example by persuading influential employees to convince others of the value of the change.
- **Coercion** involves forcing the change on reluctant groups and individuals in some cases by making them redundant, or by threatening them with sanctions should they fail to comply.

In summary it can be said that there will be a strong case for a change of strategy when:

- the current strategy is clearly inappropriate, and
- an alternative 'workable' strategy has been identified, supported by a well-formed plan for change, including ways of winning the support of individuals and groups within the organisation.

```
KEY WORDS

Radical change                Refreezing
Incremental change            Building the vision
Change agents                 Reviewing where we are now
Punctuated equilibrium        Constructing the plan
Sigmoid Curve                 Resistance to change
Adaptive strategies           Organisational barriers
Logical incrementalism        Structural inertia
Unfreezing                    Individual barriers
Changing
```

Further reading

Johnson, G., and Scholes, K., Chapter 11, *Exploring Corporate Strategy*, Financial Times/Prentice Hall, sixth edition 2000.

Pettinger, R., Chapter 12, *Introduction to Management*, third edition, 2000.

Schermerhorn, J.R., Hunt, J.G. & Osborn, R.N., Chapter 20, *Managing Organisational Behaviour*, John Wiley, seventh edition, 2001.

Thompson, J.L.,Chapter 1, *Strategic Management*, Thomson Business Press, fourth edition, 2000.

Further references

Handy, C., *The Empty Raincoat, Making Sense of the Future*, Hutchinson, 1995.

Lewin, K., Group decision and social change, in G.E. Swanson, T.M. Newcomb and L.E. Hartley, eds, *Readings in Social Psychology*, Holt, Rinehart and Winston, 1952.

Quinn, J.B., *Strategies for Change: Logical Incrementalism*, Irwin, 1980.

Stacey, R., *Strategic Management and Organisational Dynamics*, Pitman 1993.

Useful websites

www.iceland.co.uk
www.futurenet.co.uk

Essay topics

1. (a) To what extent should managing change be seen as a one-off
       process?   [10 marks]

(b) How might change management involve changing:
   (i) the culture of an organisation
   (ii) the structure of the organization   [10 marks]

2. (a) Give examples of internal and external barriers to change in managing organisational change.   [10 marks]
  (b) Explain how managers might overcome two of the internal barriers to change that you have outlined in (a).   [10 marks]

Data response – Changing culture at Corus

Corus came into being as a result of a merger between British Steel and the Dutch company Hoogovens on 6 October 1999.

Immediately it was decided to change the culture of the organisation to make it more customer focused. Corus has been seeking to create high performance teams within its business units in order to improve performance and particularly to build stronger relationships with customers. A key change that has taken place in organisational structure has been in the organisation of sales accounts teams. Before the merger, Corus operated with product-based sales teams operating from four different geographical locations. The new emphasis has been on bringing the management of sales to a centralised area at Scunthorpe. Now empowered sales account managers have the responsibility for managing accounts with individual customers. The new account manager is entrusted to know all aspects of the business aided by the latest information and communications technology systems. What this means is that a customer like British Waterways will deal with one Corus account manager rather than having to buy different types of steel from a range of sales staff and locations as was the case in the past.

While it has been pursuing this strategy, it has been faced with an external environment which contains many hostile factors. The major hostile factor has been the strength of the £ and the weakness of the euro which has made it particularly difficult for UK manufacturers. Corus is one of the UK's top ten exporters, its aim is to retain regular customers' existing orders and to win new ones in a competitive market place, which is not helped by the weakness of the euro.

Corus has had to develop an extensive process for managing change particularly in its sales force. it had to move from a situation in which there was a hierarchical structure in which many of the sales staff expected to be told what to do. Managing change has involved a process of breaking staff away from the 'comfort zone' of behaving in a certain way, 'If you do what you have always done, you get what you always got' to developing new ways of working in which the new sales account managers have considerable responsibility: to sign off deals and to negotiate contracts for example.

An important aspect of the change was that of relocating employees to Scunthorpe: previously the sales force had been located across the country. The new staff needed to be re-trained in new areas so that they could work with new products and new systems. Not everyone was prepared to make the move or to make the change in the way they worked. Training programmes therefore had to be introduced to familiarise people with a range of products that were new to them, new markets, and new ways of dealing with people.

One of the major difficulties faced in the early days of introducing the changes was the sheer volume of learning that needed to take place, as individuals had to take on board a lot of new information and ways of working.

Another barrier to change was that of 'invisible walls' that existed between people within the unit. Previously contact had been made over the phone between people at different locations and dealing with different products. Now these people were working in an open plan office at the same location in Scunthorpe but at first there was still a reluctance to share ideas and to develop common systems – many people wanted to continue working with the old patterns.

1. Identify two internal barriers to change faced by Corus change agents in managing change in the case study. [2 marks]
2. Explain how these barriers might have been overcome. [6 marks]
3. How might changes in the external environment make it difficult for managers to ensure the success of the changes? [4 marks]
4. How might Corus managers seek to refreeze the changes once they had been implemented? [8 marks]

Chapter Nine

Developing a global strategy

'Ours is now a globe whose furthermost corner has been conquered by technology and opened to economic exploitation; when any incident whatsoever, regardless of where and when it occurs, can be communicated to the rest of the world at any desired speed.'
W.E. Scheuerman

Globalisation can be defined as the increasing integration of markets for goods, services and capital. Globalisation involves an acceleration in the expansion of international production, distribution and selling of goods into more worldwide geographical locations in response to changing demands in the marketplace. Much of this pressure for change comes from consumers – today we expect our local supermarket to supply us with exotic food products from all over the world throughout the year, and we accept it as the norm to buy consumer durables such as cars, televisions, DVD players, etc., which may have been produced in Brazil or South-East Asia. In the same way, UK companies like Cadbury-Schweppes are responding to consumer pressure throughout the globe to sell Cream Eggs, chocolate bars or tonic water in Mauritius, Malaysia or Mexico.

Businesses in the 21st century are faced with the reality of competing in a global market place. Barriers between markets have been eroded by:

- New technologies which have effectively shrunk the globe, enabling instant communications, and a vast reduction in distribution times and costs.
- The freeing up of trade between countries, by a series of economic treaties that have slashed import taxes.
- A new **global mindset** in which companies see the huge markets that exist in the key population centres of the globe as their domestic markets.
- The realisation by businesses that their once protected domestic markets are now part of the expansion strategies of their overseas rivals. Once a company starts losing business to a rival then all the advantages of producing on a large scale start to disappear.

The challenge of globalisation has been accepted by multinational and global corporations who are seizing the opportunity to enter markets that have been closed to their trading advances in the past.

A multinational company is:	A global company is:
• a highly developed international company with a deep involvement throughout the world, plus a worldwide perspective in its management and decision making • one which tailors its products to the specific needs of consumers in a particular country.	• one which manages its worldwide operations as if they were totally interconnected • one which treats each country as part of one worldwide industry • one which manufactures and sells the same products, with only minor adjustments made for individual countries around the world.

The two main factors that differentiate global corporations (**globalisation**) from multinational corporations (**internationalisation**) are:

- that each part of the business no matter in what country it is located, is an integrated segment of a worldwide network
- products are produced specifically for global distribution (a worldwide market).

The technology revolution

A technology revolution is changing the world economy and influencing how big business is done. 200 million people throughout the world were on the Internet at the end of 2000, and 500 million will be by 2002. It is estimated that by the end of 2005 nearly 60 per cent of the world's population will be online. Communication is possible to almost any part of the world, opening up a global network and creating a marketplace in areas that were not accessible before. Computers and WAP phones incorporating the Internet, e-mail and video conferencing are just examples of the new technological links enabling instant communication. The term the '**weightless economy**' has been applied to new transactions involving trading in modern services.

At the same time, modern air transport links have made it possible for people and goods to be rapidly transported from one part of the globe to another, while sophisticated refrigeration techniques have enabled fresh produce to be transported over vast distances from the producer to the consumer. With huge numbers of consumers having access to the television, radio and other mass media, the costs of marketing and distribution have been slashed.

Factory systems that are required to mass produce modern consumer goods can be built within months rather than years using modern technology, so that multinational and global companies can quickly build new production capacity close to their desired markets.

The freeing of world trade

The end of the 20th century saw widespread decreases in international barriers to trade as tariff barriers were progressively reduced by international agreements. The main focus for change was the **World Trade Organisation (WTO)** which was set up as a permanent body in 1995 and which sets the rules for international commerce.

The WTO was set up as the result of a number of conferences between representatives of over 130 different countries who over the years agreed to cut down on trade barriers. The main argument for cutting down trade barriers was that nations would benefit from specialising in what they do best when compared with other countries – the so-called law of **comparative advantage**. Undoubtedly volumes of goods traded on world markets has increased enormously in recent years. Of course, it is important to register opposition that exists to such an expansion of world trade. Environmentalists argue that we are using up the worlds' scarce resources at an unsustainable rate. Developing countries argue that when you start from so far behind other countries on the road to development, your best lines will rarely command high prices on world markets, so that you will never be able to generate the savings which enable you to invest in high technology industries.

The other key feature of the freeing of world trade is that countries have increasingly organised themselves into massive free trade blocs such as the European Union, and NAFTA the **North American Free Trade Agreement** between the USA, Canada and Mexico to progressively eliminate tariffs over a 10-15 year period (from 1994).

Today the world economy is dominated by three huge trading blocs referred to as 'The Triad' of North American, the European Union, and Japan and South-East Asia. It is argued that for a large modern international company to be successful, it must have a large market share in at least two of these three blocs. A global corporation needs to have a strong presence in all three blocs.

Developing a global strategy

The secret to success in all industries today is extreme sensitivity to international events and forces that are reshaping the business environment. An organisation must respond to its external environment and adjust its corporate strategy accordingly. For example, technological advances are opening up world markets to an organisation's competitors. If the organisation does not respond to this challenge then their own business will get left behind.

As corporations become more involved with the global economy, they will need to constantly review the appropriateness of their current mission and objectives. Long-term planning has to be adjusted to take into account the changes involved in the global economy.

The foundation stones for globalisation strategy are:

- **Mission** – setting out the general aim of the organisation and its purpose in relation to globalisation.
- **Objectives** – more precise statements setting out global objectives.
- **Strategies** – broad statements of intent showing the action required to achieve the objectives, e.g. outlining the broad plans for achieving global objectives.

After taking into consideration all the above, which may be seen as the basis to build future plans, the organisation then must look at its **scope** and **resources**. The scope is concerned with what they produce (global products) and where they produce (global markets), e.g. identifying their best lines and the best location for their production. They must also identify how to use their existing resources to achieve the global objectives of the organisation.

The importance of powerbrands

To be competitive in a global industry, companies are discovering that they must raise the quality of their products and reduce their prices.

Like countries, business organisations have a **comparative advantage** in their best lines. For example, the Coca-Cola Company is the best producer of Coca-Cola in the world – its advantage is based on the Coca-Cola logo, the image of the product, and marketing at globally televised events such as the Olympics and the World Cup.

Each organisation should concentrate on its best products, e.g. what it is best at producing, and forget about other marginal products. In this way vital energy and resources are channelled into specific lines, which in turn improve the efficiency of these lines, resulting in better quality products at competitive prices.

Offering a product that has a global appeal gives another advantage in the marketplace as the larger the appeal to the mass market one product has, the more sales will result and the greater the profit margin.

Another way in which the multinational or global corporation may gain an advantage in the marketplace is by **strategic alliances** and **acquisitions** to take advantage of existing businesses throughout the world to complement and expand their own product ranges.

In recent years multinational and global corporations have begun to concentrate on what they see as being their '**powerbrands**', i.e. those products in which they have the greatest competitive advantage.

For example, companies like Heinz have slimmed down the range of products that they produce to concentrate on powerbrands, e.g. products like Heinz tomato ketchup and Heinz baby foods. They realise that if their strategy is to dominate global markets in the products that they have the greatest competitive advantage in, then they must divest themselves of other lines. Selling off non-powerbrands raises the funds necessary to develop the powerbrands on a global scale (see boxed text below).

Unilever's powerbrand strategy

Unilever was formed in 1930 when the Dutch margarine company Margarine Unie merged with British soapmaker Lever Brothers.

Unilever NV and Unilever PLC are the parent companies of what is today one of the largest consumer goods businesses in the world. Since 1930, the two companies have operated as one, linked by a series of agreements and shareholders that participate in the prosperity of the whole business. Unilever's corporate centres are London and Rotterdam.

International by design, Unilever have deep roots in many countries. Local companies are predominantly run by local people in tune with their local communities and who understand their needs and values – a truly 'multi-local multinational'.

Today Unilever's product range is vast and diverse in the areas of foods and home and personal care, e.g. skin care, oral care, personal wash and prestige products.

Products are clustered in the following areas:

- culinary products
- frozen foods
- ice-cream
- tea-based beverages
- spreads and cooking products
- household care
- deodorants
- hair care
- fragrances
- diagnostics
- professional cleaning
- laundry.

Worldwide sales are over £30billion and the company employs nearly 250,000 people worldwide. The company invests around £600 million in technology and innovation each year and spends £3.5billion on marketing its brands.

Unilever's powerbrands include Magnum ice-cream, Dover personal wash and Lipton tea – brands which are known and trusted by millions of consumers around the world.

In 1999 Unilever decided on a strategy of cutting back on its portfolio of 1,600 brands to concentrate on just 400 leading powerbrands. These powerbrands were chosen on the basis of the strength of their current consumer appeal and their prospects for sustained growth. Between 1999 and 2004 the company is investing £1billion in extra marketing support for these powerbrands with the objective of seeing growth rates in these brands of 6 per cent per annum.

To support the powerbrand strategy, Unilever has developed supporting strategies of:

- the development of e-business, to improve brand communications and develop direct relationships with customers
- restructuring the company into 12 business groups each with the responsibility to meet the corporate centre objectives. Regional strategies have been developed to support the global strategy.

Unilever has set out its corporate purpose (which includes its mission) as:

'Our purpose in Unilever is to meet the everyday needs of people everywhere – to anticipate the aspirations of our consumers and customers and to respond creatively and competitively with branded products and services which raise the quality of life.

Our deep roots in local cultures and markets around the world and our unparalleled inheritance is the foundation for our future growth. We will bring our wealth of knowledge and international expertise to the service of local consumers – a truly multi-local multinational.

Our long-term success requires a total commitment to exceptional standards of performance and productivity, to working together effectively and to a willingness to embrace new ideas and learn continuously.

We believe that to succeed requires the highest standards of corporate behaviour towards our employees, consumers and the societies and world in which we live.'

The Unilever case study provides a good example of the way in which a very large multinational company has developed a global strategy. Because Unilever has increased the geographical scope of its strategies, it has needed the resources to extend its operations on a global scale. This has involved both finding resources internally from profits and selling off existing (non-powerbrand) businesses, and through the acquisition of other companies producing brands that best fit with their existing portfolio of core products. For example, in 1999 Unilever made 27 acquisitions throughout the world including those listed in Table 5.

Table 5 Unilever acquisitions since 1999

Brand	Country	Product area
Varela SA	Columbia	Home and personal care
Mountain Cream	China and Hong Kong	Ice-cream
Beijing Tea Processing Factory	China	Tea
Sociedad Industrial Dominicana	Dominican Republic	Home and personal care and ice-cream
Miro Aebe	Greece	Tomato products
Rossell	India	Tea plantation
Selecta Dairy Products Inc.	Philippines	Ice-cream
Slotts & Knockens	Sweden	Culinary brands

Unilever are strategically planning their path from being a multinational corporation into a global corporation. They are using technology to do this by establishing a worldwide communication network. Their 400 top brands have been chosen for their global appeal.

In this chapter we have focused on one of the most significant types of competitive strategy that large companies are involved in today. Globalisation is a reality for companies like Unilever, Nestlé, Cadbury-Schweppes, Coca-Cola, Pepsi-Co, Nike, Adidas, Manchester United and many other players. Should they fail to respond to globalisation they stand to go the way of the dinosaurs.

KEY WORDS

Globalisation	Mission
Global mindset	Objectives
Multinational company	Strategies
Global company	Scope
Internationalisation	Resources
Weightless economy	Comparative advantage
World Trade Organisation	Strategic alliances
Comparative advantage	Acquisitions
North American Free Trade Agreement	Powerbrands
The Triad	Corporate purpose

Further reading

Johnson, G., and Scholes, K., Chapter 3, *Exploring Corporate Strategy*, sixth edition, 2000, Financial Times/Prentice Hall.

Joyce, P. and Woods, A., Chapter 8, *Essential Strategic Management*, Butterworth Heinemann, 1996.

Schermerhorn, J.R., Hunt, J.G. and Osborn, R.N., Chapter 3, *Managing Organisational Behaviour*, John Wiley, seventh edition, 2001.

Wheelen,T.L. and Hunger, J.D., *Strategic Management and Business Policy, Entering 21st Century Global Society*, seventh edition, Addison Wesley Longman, 2001.

Useful websites

Unilever website: www.unilever.com

Heinz website: www.heinz.com

Essay topics

1. (a) Why is it important for large business organisations to develop global strategies in the 21st century?   [12 marks]
    (b) Why is it important to build flexibility into global strategies?
                                                                [8 marks]
2. Describe how one well-known multinational organisation has developed a global strategy?   [10 marks]
    To what extent has this global strategy been shaped by competition?   [10 marks]

Data response question

Coca-Cola and P&G join forces in new juice and snacks venture

Coca-Cola, the soft drinks giant, and Procter & Gamble, the consumer products group, are forming a stand-alone juice and snack company, which will unite Coca-Cola's Minute Maid juices, Hi-C, Five-Alive and Fruitopia drinks with P&G's Pringles snack crisps and Sunny Delight beverages.

Each company will own 50 per cent of the yet to be named venture, which is expected to have annual sales of more than $4bn (£2.8bn). Don Short, a 24-year Coca-Cola veteran, was named chief executive.

'This new company will focus all of its resources on becoming the global leader in innovative snacks and nutritional beverages,' Coca-Cola's chairman and chief executive, Doug Daft, and Procter & Gamble president and chief executive AG Lafley, said in a statement.

The ventures marries Coca-Cola's quest to expand its non-carbonated beverage lineup with P&G's need to boost lagging crisp and juice sales. P&G has suffered from shrinking sales that have prompted some analysts to say the company needed to exit the snack and juice business.

Proctor & Gamble's food and beverage sales fell 12 per cent to $2.23bn in the six months ended 31 December compared with a year ago, with earnings down 18 per cent.

At the same time, Coca-Cola faces the prospect of lagging behind its rival PepsiCo in noncarbonated beverages, which are growing faster than the carbonated segment, where Coca-Cola leads. It recently lost out to PepsiCo in a bid to buy South Beach Beverage, the drinks maker. Pepsi is also buying Gatorade, the sports drink.

The new company will be able to take advantage of P&G's research and development capabilities, while also putting P&G products into Coca-Cola's worldwide distribution system.

The new company will have 15 manufacturing facilities and about 6000 employees, the companies said.

The Independent, 22 February 2001

1. Why have P&G and Coca-Cola set up this joint venture?

[10 marks]

2. To what extent can the move by Coca-Cola be described as a competitive strategy? [5 marks]

3. How might it be possible to judge the success of the joint venture in future years? [5 marks]

Conclusion

There can be no doubt that an understanding of the nature of corporate strategy is one of the most important topics in business. We have seen in this book that corporate strategies are the big plans that affect the whole organisation. Corporate strategy involves top-level decision making and senior management. Increasingly it will need also to become the concern of everyone in the organisation.

Strategic plans determine the priority given to the various concerns and functions of an organisation. For example, if areas such as business ethics, concern for the environment, human resource management and so on, are to be given significant weighting in business policy then they will need to be given prominence in the mission statement and objectives of the organisation. Fortunately, in recent years we have seen enlightened businesses giving greater prominence to these areas partially as a result of increasing stakeholder pressure from government, consumers and the community.

However, most businesses are all too aware of the competitive environment in which they operate and in a competitive climate, strategies are very much tied up with survival, and the maintenance of sufficient profits to reinvest to retain competitive advantage. Strategies are and will continue to be driven by competition.

What is certain in the 21st century is that the environment in which business operates is becoming increasingly turbulent. Organisations increasingly operate in an era of change in which we see:

- rapid changes in technology which increase efficiency, productivity, speed of production and consumer power
- global interconnections between people on an unprecedented scale
- intense competition which has been intensified by globalisation and rapid developments in technology
- change in all manner of environmental variables – so that change creates a climate of uncertainty
- increased speed of change – in technology, in globalisation, in competition.

All of the above factors create a highly complex organisational environment. Strategic planning is important in helping organisations to manage these changes successfully but strategic managers must recognise that their strategies must be based on flexibility.

The development of successful strategies in the future will be based on new types of thinking. Increasingly, organisations will need to be based on the sharing of knowledge and the participation of more and more people in creating plans and helping to formulate strategy. At the same time, organisations will need to develop new structures and patterns to encourage innovation and creativity. Teamwork is already becoming the new way of working of many modern organisations allowing joint efforts, the free flow of ideas and maximum commitment to seeing strategies succeed. In a complex, changing environment organisations will benefit from drawing on diversity – it will be a strength for the organisation to be made up of many different types of people whose views are valued. Finally, the organisation of the future will need to have a strong value system which reflects the values of stakeholders working together rather than a narrow managerial perspective. With this shared value system and sense of purpose the new organisation will be best placed to create successful strategies for a new world.

Case studies in corporate strategy

Having examined the key processes involved in identifying, choosing and managing corporate strategies it is useful to examine examples of strategies chosen by well known organisations in recent times.

Strategy formulation is a dynamic discipline requiring complex thinking involving an element of risk, particularly because of the changing environment in which organisations operate. Today, organisational strategies are continually on the move, reflecting the way in which most organisations are having to shift their focus of interest to keep in step with the changing market place.

An element of risk

The problem of choosing a strategy is that there is always an element of risk. Building a strategy involves considerable investment of resources, so if a poor choice is made, then this can be disastrous for an organisation.

Senior managers play the key role in selecting the appropriate strategy. Stakeholders will scrutinise the choice of strategy in detail. Discontented stakeholders can quickly show their disapproval about the strategic choices made – for example, shareholders may sell their shares, leading to a fall in value of a company which can then lead to a take-over bid.

The changing environment

The wider organisational environment is continually in flux, making it difficult for businesses to plan ahead. In such a world, the map to the future cannot be drawn in advance. We cannot know enough to set forth a meaningful vision or to plan productively. In fact, engaging in such activities in the belief that we can predict the future and, to a degree, control it, is probably both illusory and dangerous in that it allows a false and potentially debilitating sense of security. The strategic planner therefore needs to build into thinking about the future an understanding that change will occur. It is important to use PESTLE and SWOT techniques to get a clear understanding of environmental forces, but always to build in an element of surprise and a recognition of unpredictability.

The changing market place and the virtual organisation

Twenty years ago most organisations were typically associated with given product lines – a bicycle manufacturer made bicycles, a pharmaceutical company made pharmaceuticals, etc. Today, there is far more flexibility in terms of what business organisations do. Instead of thinking of a business as a producer of a given product line it is often more helpful to think of that business as a basket of resources which can be switched from one given mix of products to another in order to take advantage of market opportunities. The virtual organisation does not have to stick with its traditional lines for years and years – rather it continues with existing successes, seeks new opportunities for success and divests itself of businesses where the rate of return is lowest. There are parallels here with the way in which a modern supermarket is run. Today's supermarket uses its shelf space to stock those items which give it the greatest profits per square metre. Items with a slow turnover or ones with unprofitable margins are eliminated.

The strategies of virtual organisations are focused on securing the best possible returns to stakeholders. Yesterday's bicycle manufacturer may no longer produce bicycles – it may produce something completely different. In addition the name of the business may change because its basket of resources is now focused on quite different lines.

Case Study 1 – MFI moves out of its core lines into bathrooms

Some growth strategies are concerned with moving on beyond your existing core areas – taking up opportunities in new or existing markets.

In late 2001, MFI, the furniture retailer, started selling bathrooms through 50 of its stores as it sought to expand beyond its existing core ranges of kitchens and bedrooms.

This expansion took place in July and November 2001. MFI saw the possibility of taking advantage of a market (UK bathroom furniture) which is worth £1.1bn a year. MFI's target was to register sales of £1.1m from the product addition in the first year.

The expansion was announced at a time (May 2001) that the company was enjoying a strong recovery in sales and in the share price.

Questions for discussion
1. Why do you think MFI was engaging in this growth strategy?
2. Does it make sense for organisations to develop strategies which involve expanding beyond their core strengths?
3. What elements of risk do you see as being involved in this expansion strategy?

Case Study 2 – Abbey National expands presence in market for financial services for the wealthy

Michael Porter argues that if an organisation can gain the lion's share of the market then the profits will follow – of course there are risks attached to this strategy.

In May 2001, Abbey National, the UK's second largest mortgage bank, accelerated its advance into financial services for the wealthy with a £106m deal to buy the upmarket telephone banking arm of Robert Fleming.

The deal boosted Abbey's share of accounts belonging to affluent clients to 16 per cent of the market, allowing it to steal a march on rivals also trying to grab new business in this profitable sector.

The new businesses added 110,000 customers to Abbey's existing 26,000 clients with an annual income of £30,000 to £100,000. The deal significantly accelerated Abbey's stated plan to achieve this level of market share within three years.

The week before HSBC and Merrill Lynch announced a £700m joint venture to enter the same market. Barclays had developed a premier banking service, giving it 17 per cent of accounts for moderate to high earners.

Before the take-over of Robert Fleming, Abbey National had 3 per cent of the 'mass affluent' market. The take-over increased Abbey National's market share to 14 per cent. Most of the new business was made up of customers' primary accounts, which banks covet for potential cross-sales of other products to clients.

Questions for discussion

1. Why is the 'mass affluent' market so attractive for businesses operating in the financial services market?
2. What do you see as being Abbey National's main objective with regard to this market?
3. How do the take-over strategies help it to achieve this objective?
4. What do you see as being the risks involved in this strategy?
5. How might Abbey National secure the resources to support this strategy? What are the implications for the nature of their existing business?

Case Study 3 – Capital Radio set to expand

As the environment in which business organisations operate changes they are frequently forced into adapting to this environment or face the danger of losing out to rivals who are already adapting to the changed environment.

Capital Radio, Britain's biggest radio group, announced in May 2001 that it would be expanding its interests (buying other radio and media interests) despite a drop in profits of about 25 per cent to £30m.

In response to a Government White Paper on cross-media ownership due to become law in 2002, it is likely that there will be a number of mergers and take-overs involving Britain's several dozen radio groups.

The chief executive of Capital stated on national television that he saw there being a significant consolidation opportunity for Capital and predicted that two or three UK radio groups would come to dominate the market. He predicted that new media ownership legislation was likely to give rise to a greater cross-media concentration, allowing, for example, television groups to own radio outlets. Increasingly different media are converging as a result of digital technology. Different types of media are increasingly becoming closer substitutes.

One of the main reasons for Capital's fall in profits was that while sales revenues had been rising the cost of investing in digital and internet investment had more than offset this increase.

Questions for discussion
1. Why do you think that Capital Radio was talking about expanding its media interests?
2. To what extent is this a response to a change in the external environment?
3. What would be the dangers in not expanding its media interests?

Case Study 4 – Retrenchment at Marks and Spencer

Retrenchment is the process of cutting back activities away from what are seen to be niche or peripheral markets. The purpose here is to better enable an organisation to concentrate on its core activities to better focus its energies.

At the turn of the new millennium it was apparent that Marks and Spencer, which up until that point had perhaps been this country's most respected business, was in difficulty. In particular the criticism was levelled that it had lost touch with customers and that the image of the company was out-dated. In an attempt to re-invent itself the company has been rolling out a series of 'new concept stores' selling new ranges and with a new look to them including the sale of designer labels.

At the same time a radical plan was set in motion to close M&S's continental European stores, sell its American business and re-focus on the UK. The American and European stores were seen as being peripheral to M&S's future and a drain on resources.

Questions for discussion
1. How can the M&S strategy outlined above be described as retrenchment?
2. What do you see as being the main objectives behind the retrenchment strategy?
3. Why might such a strategy involve considerable dangers?

Case Study 5 – Restructuring to avoid further losses

Designing effective corporate strategies is all about enabling an organisation to move forward. In recent years a number of business gurus have suggested that the prime objective of a business is to survive. At times the organisation needs to restructure and cut out loss making activities if the core of the organisation is to survive and move forward.

In May 2001 the car maker Vauxhall announced losses of around £190m resulting from heavy restructuring costs involving the ending of car production at the Luton site.

The UK subsidiary of General Motors was also hit hard by increased pressure on new car prices and a decline in output caused by falling demand for the Vectra model.

The company made operating profits of about £25m in 2000 but these were wiped out by one-off charges of about £200m to cover the costs of its withdrawal from Luton.

Output from Vauxhall's Luton and Ellesmere Port plants fell by more than 10 per cent in 2000. The reduction was largely due to falling sales of the Vectra which was being replaced by a new model at the start of 2002. The strength of sterling also affected exports to the continent. Vauxhall exported almost 60 per cent of production and car derived vans in 2000.

General Motors as a whole lost a total of £180m in Europe in 2000 compared with a profit of £300m in 1999. The sharp reversal was one of the reasons for the cutback in production which also affected plants on the Continent.

Questions for discussion
1. What factors have led General Motors to restructure?
2. Why was it decided to close down the Luton plant?
3. How does this restructuring programme help Vauxhall to survive?
4. What effect will these changes have on the structure of General Motors?

Case Study 6 – Taking a total stakeholder view of corporate strategy

Organisations today are more aware than ever that they need to serve a variety of stakeholders if they are to earn a licence to operate, and to win the ongoing support of their customers, their employees, the government and other key stakeholders.

Nowhere is this more true than in developing strategies which involve building a concern for the environment. Increasingly organisations are realising the importance of developing strategies based on a Triple Bottom Line. The key concept here is that organisations derive their licence to operate not just by satisfying shareholders through improved profits and dividends (the economic bottom line), but by simultaneously satisfying other stakeholders in society (employees, customers, communities, etc.) through improved performance in terms of their social and environmental bottom lines, for example by engaging in fair trade with suppliers, by empowering employees, by carrying out environmental audits, by benchmarking against the leading environmental standards available, etc.

The Co-operative Bank is at the forefront of environmental sustainability and prides itself on being socially and ecologically sound. The whole basis of the Co-operative bank is to be ethically sound, and this has been their key area of competitive advantage over the last ten years. This strategy has been progressively rolled out, evaluated and improved, since the organisation carried out a study in the 1990s which indicated that there was a niche in the market for an ethically and ecologically sound bank. The strategy also fitted with the organisation's history as part of the co-operative movement.

The Co-operative Bank has made a clear stance on all ethical policies and this has boosted the organisation's public profile and profits. In 2000, they boosted their profit before tax to £96.3 million, 8.7 per cent higher than the previous year.

The Co-operative Bank signalled its intentions with regard to the environment with the creation of an ecological mission statement which states:

> We will encourage business customers to take a pro-active stance on the Ecological Impact of their own activities and will invest in companies that avoid repeated damage to the environment.

This mission statement spearheads a raft of policies and programmes employed by the bank. They explain why it is important for all companies to develop sustainable strategies in the following terms:

- Nature cannot withstand a progressive build-up of waste derived from the earth's crust.
- Nature cannot withstand a progressive build-up of society's waste, particularly artificial persistent substances which it cannot degrade into harmless materials.
- The productive area of nature must not be diminished in quality (diversity) and quantity (volume) and must be enabled to grow.
- Society must utilise energy and resources in a sustainable, equitable and efficient manner.

The Co-operative Bank have highlighted their main responsibilities as consisting of:

- ecological sustainability
- social responsibility
- delivering value

The diagram shows that the bank places equal emphasis on delivering value to their customers as on creating a sustainable business ecologically and socially.

Given the mission of the organisation, the Co-operative Bank has been able to create policies and systems which determine the way in which the organisation works. These are set out in five main areas.

1. Financial services – they actively encourage their business customers to take a pro-active stance on the environment, and the bank will only invest in other companies who do not repeatedly damage the environment.
2. Management systems – the Co-op bank assess their ecological impact as a company, and set themselves clear targets to improve and monitor this.
3. Purchasing and outsourcing – the bank welcomes suppliers whose activities are compatible with their ecological and ethical mission statements.
4. Support – they actively lend their support to ecological projects, and try to develop partnerships with companies who contribute to a sustainable society.
5. Legislation – the Co-operative bank adheres to all government legislation concerning the environment.

To make sure that the company is adhering to all its policies, they have set in place a mechanism whereby each year they are audited to ensure that they keep all their promises. This audit is internal and has highlighted many key areas to the firm, which can be built on and developed further.

Questions for discussion

1. How has the Co-operative Bank been able to take advantage of a changing market place?
2. What is meant by a Triple Bottom Line?
3. How is attention to the Triple Bottom Line likely to help an organisation to satisfy a range of stakeholders?
4. Why was it important for the Co-operative Bank to create an ecological mission statement?
5. How has the mission statement helped the organisation to design appropriate policies?

Case Study 7 – Constructing a Decision Tree to help in choosing a strategy

Decision trees are so named because of the way in which they separate out into branches (outcomes) from an original root (a decision). Decision trees are a technique for tracing through all the known outcomes of a particular decision in order to draw out the possible consequences.

Decision trees can set out the possible consequences to a firm deciding to employ a new strategy. Decision trees used in business will also set out to calculate the probability of each event (branch). The probability of each event is then multiplied by the expected return (profit or loss) resulting from that outcome to arrive at an expected value.

(In a decision tree diagram a square represents a decision, and a circle represents a chance event, i.e. a situation in which one of two or more events will follow).

In the example below Novelty Websites PLC is considering a new strategy, e.g. launching a new improved service to customers. Research indicates an 80 per cent chance of success for the new service (i.e. a probability of 0.8). Because probabilities add up to 1 there is therefore a 0.2 chance of failure.

To make a decision using this tool, estimates need to be made of costs and returns involved with the project.

In this example,

- The launch of the new service will cost £20 million.
- The success of new service will generate £30 million of positive net cash flows.
- If the service fails this will only generate £6 million.
- If Novelty Websites does nothing (i.e. doesn't launch) there will be no movements in net cash.

The decision tree will look like the following:

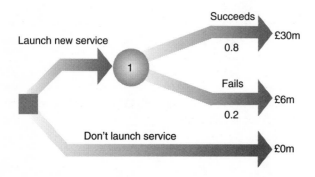

In order to work out whether the new strategy will be a success it is now necessary to calculate the expected value of the return on the strategy.

We know that there is:

A 0.8 chance of achieving a return of £30m, and
A 0.2 chance of achieving a return of £6m.

We can then work out the expected value by working out an average weighted outcome:

i.e. £30m × 0.8 = £24m
£6m × 0.2 = £1.2m

Therefore the expected value is £25.2m.

We can now redraw the decision tree to show the expected value at the chance event. Clearly this is a preferable option to that of not launching the new service which would have yielded £0m.

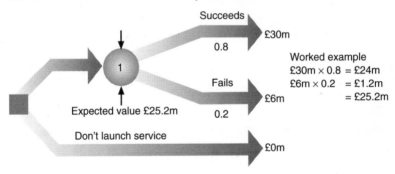

Of course, in the real world organisations are faced with a menu of strategic options, and it is then possible to work out a range of expected values from each strategy. The option with the highest expected value can then be chosen.

In the real world decision tree analysis may be used for deciding on a product launch, or perhaps in deciding whether to take over another business or not. However, this approach would need to be supported by a lot more detailed qualitative information because in a highly dynamic business environment quantitative information is only of limited value – this year's probability of 0.8 may turn into next year's 0 because of rapid changes in market conditions. The calculation of the probability of a predicted outcome very much depends on the information available to a decision maker and on the decision maker's interpretation of that information. It is therefore important for the decision maker to have available as much up-to-the-minute information as possible.

Questions for discussion

1. Are decision trees more likely to be used for long-term or short-term decision making in the real world?
2. Why is it difficult to calculate probabilities in strategic decision making?
3. How useful do you think decision trees are likely to be in helping organisations to develop realistic strategies?

Case Study 8 – Acquisition to focus on best lines

Most organisations in the 21st century recognise the importance of focusing their strategies, resources and activities on those lines in which they have the greatest competitive advantage. Gone are the days when organisations sought to spread their interests over a range of different types of business activity. A focused strategy therefore involves identifying the core strengths of the business, and the key markets in which these strengths can be exploited. Companies will then acquire other businesses which best fit with the existing portfolio and strengths of the original company.

In June 2001, First Choice, the package holiday operator was actively seeking acquisition opportunities in Europe to bolster its strategy of delivering at least 50 per cent of its profits from specialist holidays by 2003.

The group, which is the UK's fourth biggest tour operator, added the Netherlands as its eighth European market in mid-June 2001 by taking over Sunrise, a Dutch travel company. First Choice was also seeking opportunities in Southern Europe, especially in France, Spain and Italy. In the early part of 2001 First Choice made a number of other acquisitions in Europe and Canada.

Questions for discussion
1. Why do you think that First Choice had decided to target specialist holidays rather than general holidays?
2. Why is First Choice expanding its presence in this sector?
3. Do you think that this is a sensible strategy?
4. What dangers are associated with pursuing this strategy?

Case Study 9 – A rebranding strategy

The brand name associated with individual products and ranges of products is more important than ever before. In a global market it is increasingly important to be able to identify brands in a positive way. The brand needs to be received positively across the globe rather than in just a few markets. Large organisations therefore carry out detailed studies of the most appropriate brand image for their business.

In late June 2001 Fujitsu, the Japanese company decided to rebrand ICL as Fujitsu. ICL had been one of the best known British technology names.

Fujitsu took the decision because it believed that the rebranding would help it to strengthen its global brand in IT. At the same time DMR Consulting, a US-based technology consultancy, was also renamed Fujitsu.

In January 2001, Fujitsu commissioned Interbrand, a consultancy, to carry out research on the ICL and Fujitsu brands among customers and staff. The outcome of that research showed a move to the Fujitsu brand was clearly favoured.

Naoyuki Akikusa, Fujitsu's president and chief executive, said he believed it was the right time to switch ICL and DMR to the Fujitsu name and work under a unified brand and common mindset to deliver a full range of globally consistent yet locally attuned services to satisfy customer needs in the future.

Questions for discussion

1. Why do you think that Fujitsu adopted the rebranding strategy?
2. What do you see as being the benefits of creating a single brand for a range of businesses?
3. What do you see as being the drawbacks of creating a single brand for a range of businesses?
4. What do you understand by the expression 'globally consistent yet locally attuned services'? How might this approach help large international businesses?

Case Study 10 – Lack of flexibility in global strategies

Strategies need to be constantly evaluated so that changes can be made to counteract any weaknesses. One problem of the globalisation of organisational activity is that this can cause a reduction in flexibility. Small scale and locally based organisations are much better placed to make relatively rapid adjustments in line with changes in local conditions. However, the large global corporation generally creates elaborate systems and approaches to enable it to manage effectively over a wide geographical area. This may hinder the flexibility of such an organisation particularly where demand for products is subject to fluctuation.

In June 2001 a shoppers' backlash against bland clothing was blamed as the US retail giant Gap announced a swathe of job losses.

The company decided to shed about 7 per cent of its 10,000 workforce to offset falling profits in a move which retailing analysts suggested was because the company was no longer on the pulse with its cosy, practical but ultimately middle-of-the-road designs.

Retailing analysts suggested that the 2,881-store chain, which reported a 50 per cent fall in quarterly profits in May 2001, was in danger of repeating the disastrous results of Marks & Spencer whose customers it won over at the height of its success in the late 1990s.

In addition poor results reflected a slowdown in the US economy. In an about-turn the company reversed its plans to expand staff at its San Francisco headquarters.

By June 2001 it had become evident that the globalisation pioneered by fast food restaurants and coffee bars could not be applied in the same way to global fashion retailers unable to react quickly enough in a fickle market.

In addition Gap had been at the centre of anti-capitalist demonstrations and had lost some of its fashionable image and uniqueness as a result of too rapid an expansion of new stores in 2000.

Questions for discussion

1. Why might a global strategy be more difficult to implement in fashion retailing than in other areas of business such as food manufacturing and fast food restaurants?
2. What factors in the external environment have worked against Gap's recent expansion strategy?
3. Why might an expansion strategy have been poorly thought through?
4. What are the dangers to an organisation of growing too quickly?
5. How can an organisation develop a global strategy which avoids the dangers of overstretching and overtrading?

Case Study 11 – Retrenchment to focus on most profitable lines

Although it makes sense to expand into more and more overseas markets in an era of global competition it also makes sense to retrench and focus on your best lines to avoid the pitfalls of overstretching. By selling off less profitable lines, resources can be channelled into the most profitable ones.

In June 2001, Stagecoach, the train and bus group, announced the sale of its troubled Portuguese operations as a further step in its recovery.

The company struck a deal to sell the loss-making business to another European transport group for £14m.

At the time Stagecoach Portugal ran 135 buses on a network of services to the north and west of Lisbon. The company moved into Portugal in 1995 when it acquired the business, then called Rodoviaria Lisbon.

The move to sell off Stagecoach Portugal was part of a strategy, to focus the business on its main operations in Britain and on Coach USA, its American bus business. This followed the recent disposal of Prestwick airport.

Strategists working for Stagecoach felt that the Portuguese business was consuming too much management time and would never produce adequate results for the resources it needed.

Questions for discussion
1. Did it make sense to sell off Stagecoach Portugal?
2. What could the resources acquired from the sell-off be used for?
3. Why do organisations seek to focus their strategies?

Index